SRA

Open Court Reading

Book 1

Sharing Stories

•

Kindness

•

Look Again

SRA Open Court Reading

Book 1

Program Authors

Carl Bereiter
Marilyn Jager Adams
Marlene Scardamalia
Robbie Case
Anne McKeough
Michael Pressley
Marsha Roit
Jan Hirshberg
Ann Brown
Joe Campione
Iva Carruthers
Gerald H. Treadway, Jr.

SRA

A Division of The McGraw·Hill Companies

Columbus, Ohio

Acknowledgments

Georges Borchardt, Inc.: "The Chameleon:" from A Child's Bestiary by John Gardner (New York; Alfred A. Knopf. 1977)—Copyright © 1977 by Boskydell Artists Ltd. Reprinted by permission of Georges Borchardt, Inc. for the Estate of John Gardner.

Boyds Mills Press, Inc.: "My Book!" by David L. Harrison. Text copyright © 1993 by David L. Harrison from Somebody Catch My Homework by David L. Harrison. Published by Boyds Mills Press, Inc. Reprinted by permission.

Julie Brillhart: STORY HOUR—STARRING MEGAN! by Julie Brillhart. Text and illustrations copyright © 1992 by Julie Brillhart. Reprinted with permission of the author.

Candlewick Press Inc.: **COME BACK, JACK! Copyright © 1993 Catherine and Laurence Anholt. Reproduced by permission of Candlewick Press Inc., Cambridge, MA.**

Carolrhoda Books, Inc.: How the Guinea Fowl Got Her Spots by Barbara Knutson. Copyright 1990 by Carolrhoda Books, Inc. Used by permission of the publisher. All rights reserved.

The Child's World, Inc.: ANIMAL CAMOUFLAGE by Janet McDonnell. Copyright © 1998 by The Child's World, Inc. Reprinted with permission of The Child's World, Inc.

Columbia University Press: "The Pen" from Modern Arabic Poetry, edited by Salma Khadra Jayyusi. Copyright © 1987, Columbia University Press. Reprinted with the permission of the publisher.

Dial Books for Young Readers, a division of Penguin Putnam Inc.:

AMBER ON THE MOUNTAIN by Tony Johnston, paintings by Robert Duncan. Text copyright © 1994 by Tony Johnston. Paintings copyright © 1994 by Robert Duncan. Used by permission of Dial Books for Young Readers, a division of Penguin Putnam Inc. THE WHALES' SONG by Dyan Sheldon, pictures by Gary Blythe. Text copyright © 1990 by Dyan Sheldon. Pictures copyright © 1990 by Gary Blythe. Used by permission of Dial Books for Young Readers, a division of Penguin Putnam Inc.

Flammarion: CINDERELLA by Charles Perrault. Copyright © 1977 by Flammarion. Reprinted with permission of Flammarion.

Greenwillow Books, a division of William Morrow and Company, Inc.: "Books to the Ceiling" from WHISKERS AND RHYMES by Arnold Lobel. Copyright © 1985 by Arnold Lobel. By permission of Greenwillow Books, a division of William Morrow & Company, Inc.. THE PAPER CRANE by Molly Bang. Text copyright © 1985 by Molly Garrett Bang. By permission of Greenwillow Books, a division of William Morrow & Company, Inc.. THEY THOUGHT THEY SAW HIM by Craig Kee Strete. Illustrated by Jose Aruego and Ariane Dewey. Text copyright © 1996 by Craig Kee Strete. Illustrations copyright © 1996 by Jose Aruego and Ariane Dewey. By permission of Greenwillow Books, a division of William Morrow & Company, Inc..

HarperCollins Publishers: "APRIL MEDICINE" from GINGERBREAD DAYS by JOYCE CAROL THOMAS, illustrations by FLOYD

COOPER. TEXT COPYRIGHT © 1995 BY JOYCE CAROL THOMAS. ILLUSTRATIONS COPYRIGHT © 1995 BY FLOYD COOPER. Used by permission of HarperCollins Publishers. WHAT COLOR IS CAMOUFLAGE? by CAROLYN OTTO. Used by permission of HarperCollins Publishers.

Harvard University Press: "A Word is Dead" by Emily Dickinson. Reprinted by permission of the publishers and the Trustees of Amherst College from THE POEMS OF EMILY DICKINSON, Thomas H. Johnson, ed., Cambridge, Mass.: The Belknap Press of Harvard University Press, Copyright © 1951, 1955, 1979, 1983 by the President and Fellows of Harvard College.

Hyperion Books for Children: From ALL EYES ON THE POND text, © 1994 Michael J. Rosen. Illustrations © 1994 Tom Leonard. Reprinted with permission of Hyperion Books for Children.

Alfred A. Knopf, Inc.: **TOMÁS AND THE LIBRARY LADY by Pat Mora, illustrations by Raul Colon. Text copyright © 1997 by Pat Mora. Illustrations copyright © 1997 by Raul Colon.** Reprinted by arrangement with Alfred A. Knopf, Inc.

Random Century Children's Books: THE WHALES' SONG by Dyan Sheldon, pictures by Gary Blythe. Text copyright © 1990 by Dyan Sheldon. Pictures copyright © 1990 by Gary Blythe. Reprinted with permission of Random Century Children's Books.

The Rosen Publishing Group, Inc.: SEQUOYAH, INVENTOR OF THE CHEROKEE WRITTEN LANGUAGE by Diane Shaughnessy and Jack Carpenter. Copyright © 1997 by The Rosen Publishing Group, Inc. Reprinted with permission of The Rosen

Publishing Group, Inc.

Scholastic Inc.: From THE ELVES AND THE SHOEMAKER retold by Freya Littledale, illustrated by Brinton Turkle. Copyright © 1975 by Freya Littledale and Brinton Turkle. Reprinted by permission of Scholastic Inc. From I SEE ANIMALS HIDING by Jim Arnosky. Copyright © 1995 by Jim Arnosky. Reprinted by permission of Scholastic Inc.

Simon & Schuster Books for Young Readers, Simon & Schuster Children's Publishing Division: **MUSHROOM IN THE RAIN by Mirra Ginsburg, illustrations by Jose Aruego and Ariane Dewey. *Text copyright © 1974, by Mirra Ginsburg. Illustrations copyright © 1974, by Jose Aruego and Ariane Dewey.*** Reprinted with permission of Simon & Schuster Books for Young Readers, Simon & Schuster Children's Publishing Division. All rights reserved.

Gareth Stevens Publishing: THE STORY OF THREE WHALES by Giles Whittell, illustrations by Patrick Benson. First published 1988 by Telegraph Books/Walker Books. Text copyright © 1988 by Giles Whittell. Illustrations copyright © 1988 by Patrick Benson. Reprinted with permission of Gareth Stevens Publishing.

Viking Children's Books, a division of Penguin Putnam Inc.: "Ant and the Three Little Figs" from MY BROTHER, ANT by Betsy Byars, illustrations by Marc Simont. Text copyright © 1996 by Betsy Byars. Illustrations copyright © 1996 by Marc Simont. Used by permission of Viking Children's Books, a division of Penguin Putnam Inc. CORDUROY by Don Freeman. Copyright © 1968 by Don Freeman. Used by permission of Viking Children's Books, a division of Penguin Putnam Inc.

SRA/McGraw-Hill

A Division of The McGraw-Hill Companies

Copyright © 2000 by SRA/McGraw-Hill.

Send all inquiries to:
SRA/McGraw-Hill
8787 Orion Place
Columbus, Ohio 43240

Printed in the United States of America.

ISBN 0-02-830952-9

4 5 6 7 8 9 VHP 04 03 02 01 00

Program Authors

Carl Bereiter, Ph.D.
University of Toronto

Marilyn Jager Adams, Ph.D.
BBN Technologies

Michael Pressley, Ph.D.
University of Notre Dame

Marsha Roit, Ph.D.
National Reading Consultant

Robbie Case, Ph.D.
University of Toronto

Anne McKeough, Ph.D.
University of Toronto

Jan Hirshberg, Ed.D.

Marlene Scardamalia, Ph.D.
University of Toronto

Ann Brown, Ph.D.
University of California at Berkeley

Joe Campione, Ph.D.
University of California at Berkeley

Iva Carruthers, Ph.D.
Northeastern Illinois University

Gerald H. Treadway, Jr., Ed.D.
San Diego State University

Table *of* Contents

UNIT 1

Sharing Stories 12

Come Back, Jack! 14
humorous fiction written and illustrated by Catherine and Laurence Anholt

Meet the Author and the Illustrator, Catherine and Laurence Anholt 30

Theme Connections 31

Story Hour—Starring Megan! 32
realistic fiction written and illustrated by Julie Brillhart

Meet the Author and Illustrator, Julie Brillhart ..50

Theme Connections 51

My Book! 52
a poem written by David L. Harrison *illustrated by* Anna Rich

Ant and the Three Little Figs 54
humorous fiction written by Betsy Byars *illustrated by* Marc Simont

Meet the Author, Betsy Byars

Meet the Illustrator, Marc Simont 62

Theme Connections 63

Books to the Ceiling 64
a poem written and illustrated by Arnold Lobel

Tomás and the Library Lady 66

realistic fiction written by Pat Mora
illustrated by Raul Colón

Meet the Author, Pat Mora

Meet the Illustrator, Raul Colón 86

Theme Connections 87

Fine Art 88

Sequoyah: Inventor of the Cherokee Written Language 90

biography written by Diane Shaughnessy
and Jack Carpenter
illustrated by Sandy Rabinowitz

Meet the Authors, Diane Shaughnessy
and Jack Carpenter

Meet the Illustrator, Sandy Rabinowitz 110

Theme Connections 111

The Pen 112

a poem written by Muhammad al-Ghuzzi

A Word Is Dead 113

a poem written by Emily Dickinson
illustrated by Ruth Flanigan

Amber on the Mountain 114

realistic fiction written by Tony Johnston
illustrated by Robert Duncan

Meet the Author, Tony Johnston

Meet the Illustrator, Robert Duncan 144

Theme Connections 145

Bibliography 146

Table of Contents

UNIT 2

Kindness 148

Mushroom in the Rain 150
a fantasy retold by Mirra Ginsburg
illustrated by José Aruego and Ariane Dewey

Meet the Author, Mirra Ginsburg

Meet the Illustrators, José Aruego
and Ariane Dewey 160

Theme Connections 161

The Elves and the Shoemaker 162
a folktale retold by Freya Littledale
illustrated by Brinton Turkle

Meet the Author, Freya Littledale

Meet the Illustrator, Brinton Turkle 178

Theme Connections 179

The Paper Crane 180
fiction written and illustrated by Molly Bang

🎗 *Boston Globe-Horn Book Award*

Meet the Author and Illustrator, Molly Bang ... 196

Theme Connections 197

Fine Art 198

Corduroy 200
*a fantasy written and
illustrated by* Don Freeman

8

Meet the Author and Illustrator, Don Freeman .216

Theme Connections 217

April Medicine 218

a poem written by Joyce Carol Thomas
illustrated by Floyd Cooper

The Story of Three Whales 220

a true adventure story written by Giles Whittell
illustrated by Patrick Benson

Meet the Author, Giles Whittell

Meet the Illustrator, Patrick Benson 240

Theme Connections 241

The Whales' Song 242

fiction written by Dyan Sheldon
illustrated by Gary Blythe

🎖 *Kate Greenaway Medal*

Meet the Author, Dyan Sheldon

Meet the Illustrator, Gary Blythe 258

Theme Connections 259

Cinderella 260

a fairy tale retold by Fabio Coen
illustrated by Lane Yerkes

Meet the Author, Fabio Coen

Meet the Illustrator, Lane Yerkes 272

Theme Connections 273

Bibliography 274

Table of Contents

UNIT 3

Look Again 276

I See Animals Hiding 278
informational essay written and illustrated by Jim Arnosky

Meet the Author and Illustrator, Jim Arnosky ...290
Theme Connections 291

Animal Camouflage 292
nonfiction written by Janet McDonnell

Meet the Author, Janet McDonnell 316
Theme Connections 317

What Color Is Camouflage? 318
nonfiction written by Carolyn Otto
illustrated by Megan Lloyd

Meet the Author, Carolyn Otto
Meet the Illustrator, Megan Lloyd 340
Theme Connections 341

Fine Art 342

They Thought They Saw Him 344
fiction written by Craig Kee Strete
illustrated by José Aruego and Ariane Dewey

Meet the Author, Craig Kee Strete
Meet the Illustrators, José Aruego
and Ariane Dewey 356
Theme Connections 357

The Chameleon 358

poem written by John Gardner

illustrated by Susan Nethery

Caterpillar 359

poem written by Christina Rossetti

illustrated by Susan Nethery

How the Guinea Fowl Got Her Spots 360

a Swahili folktale retold and illustrated by Barbara Knutson

🏅 *Minnesota Book Award*

Meet the Author and Illustrator,
Barbara Knutson .378

Theme Connections 379

All Eyes on the Pond 380

poem written by Michael J. Rosen

illustrated by Tom Leonard

Meet the Author, Michael J. Rosen

Meet the Illustrator, Tom Leonard 396

Theme Connections 397

Bibliography 398

Writer's Handbook 400

Glossary 457

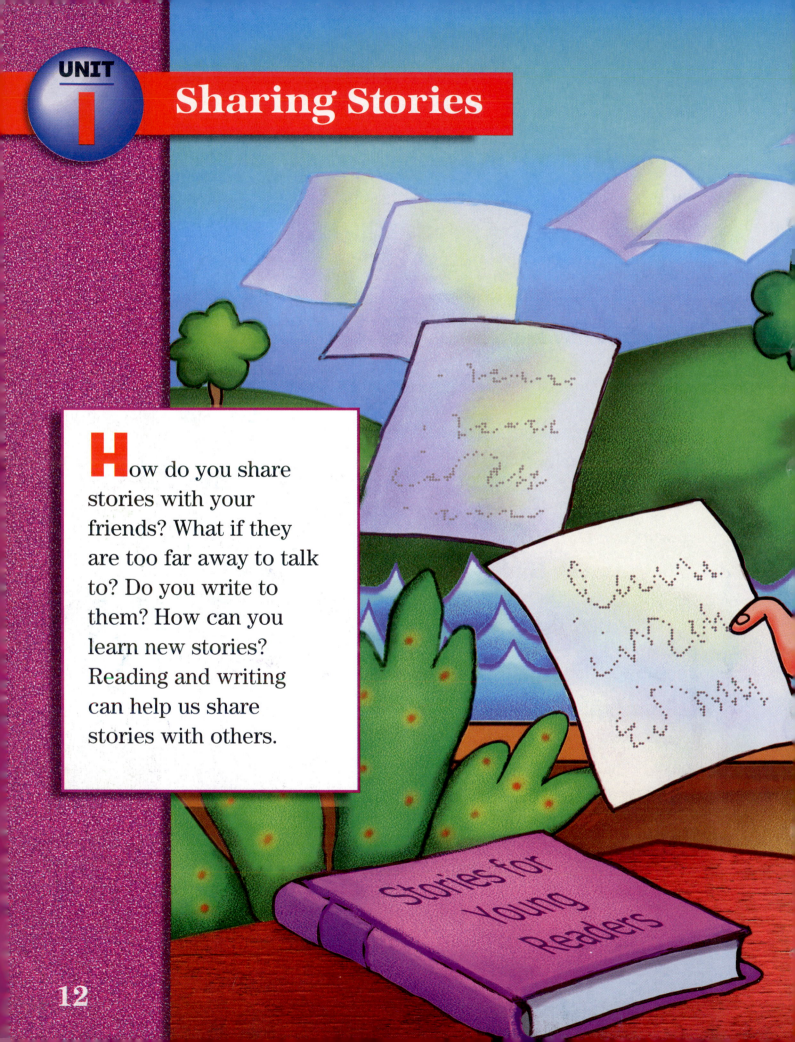

UNIT I

Sharing Stories

How do you share stories with your friends? What if they are too far away to talk to? Do you write to them? How can you learn new stories? Reading and writing can help us share stories with others.

Stories for Young Readers

Come Back, Jack!

by Catherine and Laurence Anholt

There was once a little girl who didn't like books. Her mom liked books. Her dad liked books. Her brother, Jack, *loved* books, and he couldn't even read.

"Books are boring," the little girl said. And she went out into the yard to find a real adventure.

"Keep an eye on Jack!" called the little girl's mother as Jack sat down with his book on the grass.

The little girl searched for something
exciting in the garden. She didn't find much.
When she turned around, Jack wasn't
looking at his book . . .

. . . he was crawling *inside* it!

"Come back, Jack!" called the little girl.

But Jack was already gone.

She crawled in after him.

Inside the book was a steep green hill, and at the bottom someone was crying.

"Oh no, he's hurt himself!" said the little girl.

18

But it wasn't Jack crying at the bottom of the hill. It was Jill.

"Jack fell down—and now he's run away," Jill said.

"Oh dear!" said the little girl. "Come back, Jack!"

The little girl hadn't gone far when she saw a strange crowd standing outside a house.

"This is the house that Jack built," said a cow with a crumpled horn.

"Jack isn't old enough to build houses," said the little girl. "He can't even read yet."

"But he's a clever lad," said the cow.
"Nimble and quick, too. Just watch him jump
over that candlestick!"

"Oh dear," said the little girl . . .

"COME BACK, JACK!"

The little girl found herself up in the clouds. She couldn't see Jack. What she could see was a huge castle with its enormous door wide open.

The little girl crept through the castle door—and there was Jack, sitting in a corner, eating a Christmas pie. She was just about to tell him to take out his thumb and eat politely, when the whole castle began to shake.

A great voice roared:

"FEE FI FO FUM,
I'D REALLY LIKE TO
EAT SOMEONE!"

The little girl took hold of Jack's hand,
and they ran out of the castle as quickly as
they could. But the giant had seen them.

"FUM FO FEE FI,
I WANT THOSE
CHILDREN IN A PIE!"

Just in time, they found a beanstalk
growing up through the clouds. They started
to climb down it, but the giant was getting
closer. He was about to grab them when . . .

. . . they reached the end of the book and
tumbled out into their very own backyard.

The giant's huge, hairy hand stretched out
after them, but Jack banged the book shut.

From inside the book came a faraway roar:

"FEE FI FO FUM,
NOW I'VE GONE AND HURT
MY THUMB!"

"Well," said the little girl, "perhaps books aren't boring after all!"

Then she and Jack lay on the grass, and they laughed and laughed and laughed.

Come Back, Jack!

Meet the Author and the Illustrator

Catherine and Laurence Anholt were both born in London, England. They were married in 1984 and soon after began to work together to create their own books. He usually writes the stories and she illustrates them. They want children to see themselves in the stories and to enjoy reading them.

Laurence Anholt first worked as an art teacher and wrote children's books in his free time. Many of his ideas came from listening to his three children talking. *"I want children to get the message that books are fun—it is okay to enjoy yourself."* Catherine Anholt said, *"All my drawings are from memory, although I have always intended to work from life."*

Theme Connections

Think About It

What have you learned about Sharing Stories? Here are some questions to think about:

- Did anyone show you that books are exciting and interesting? What did that person do to show you that books are fun?
- Have you ever shared a story with someone? With whom? What story did you share?
- What kinds of books do you like? Why?

Post any questions you have about Sharing Stories on the Concept/Question Board.

Record Ideas

Did you learn of any new books you want to read? Record in your Writing Journal the kinds of stories you like to read. Write down the titles of books you would like to read.

Make a Good Book List

- Write "Good Book List" at the top of a piece of paper.
- Write your name under "Good Book List."
- List five books you have read or that someone has shared with you. Then, write something you liked about each story.
- Post your list in the classroom to share with other students.

Story Hour – Starring Megan!

by Julie Brillhart

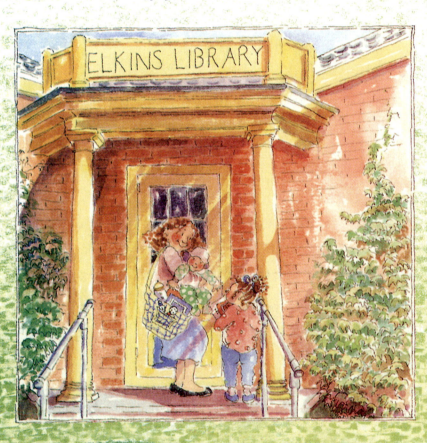

Once in awhile, when the sitter couldn't come, Megan and her baby brother, Nathan, got to spend an afternoon with their mother at the town library. Their mother was the librarian.

Megan liked the library because she had jobs to do. Her mother called her the "assistant." She put away the children's books and picked up the stuffed animals.

She decorated the bulletin board and watered the plants.

And when things got very, very busy, Megan was always ready to help with Nathan.

But most of all, Megan liked the library because she loved books and was learning to read. She couldn't wait to read every book in the whole library!

Whenever she had a chance, Megan would curl up with *Fly up High* and try to sound out the words. Often she got stuck, and her mother would help her.

Megan would sigh. "Oh, reading is so hard!"

"I know," said her mother. "But keep trying. It will come."

So Megan kept on trying. She tried at
school, in the car, at the supermarket, in the
bathtub, after dinner, and even after lights out!

She had never tried so hard at anything
before.

One time the sitter couldn't come on the day Megan's mother had story hour. "I hope Nathan sleeps through the story," said Megan's mother as the children started to arrive.

Suddenly a stuffed dinosaur came flying through the book slot in the library door. "Oh, good!" said Megan. "Andrew's here!"

Andrew came in carrying a pile of dinosaur books. "Guess what?" said Megan. "I'm learning to read!"

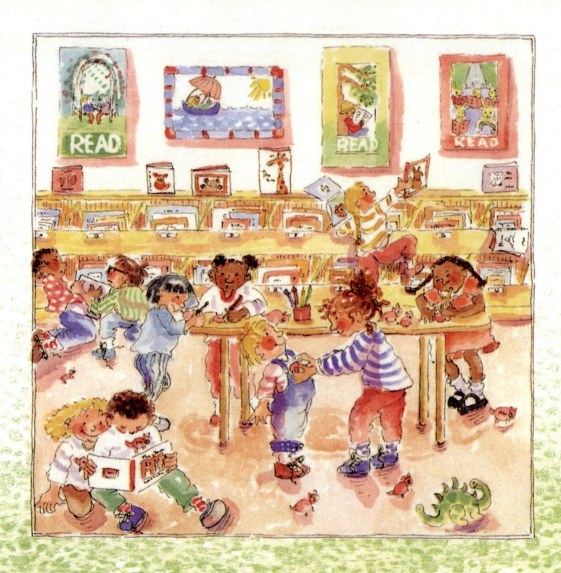

"Oh," said Andrew. "Are there any new books with pteranodons?"

"No," said Megan. "And aren't you ever going to read about *anything* else?"

Megan led the group to the children's room and passed out name tags. She helped the younger children pin on their tags.

"Welcome to story hour," said Megan's mother. "Today I would like to read—"

Right then Nathan let out a howl. Everyone turned to look.

"Just a minute," said Megan's mother. And she got up.

She tried everything to calm Nathan down, but he kept screaming.

The children were getting restless. "Please be patient," said Megan's mother. "I'm sure we will begin shortly."

While all this was going on, Megan sat thinking. Suddenly she had a great idea!

She slipped away and ran to get her favorite book.

Megan sat down in front of all the children. She felt a little scared. "I would like to read *Fly up High*," she said.

Everyone looked at her in amazement. The room became very quiet, and Nathan even stopped crying. Megan began to read.

She read on and on. She showed the children the pictures, just the way her mother did. She got stuck on a few words, but she kept going. Nobody seemed to notice when she made a mistake.

She read the whole book!

The children all clapped and cheered. And so did some moms and dads who had come in. Megan felt terrific!

She looked over at her mom. "I did it!"
Megan said.

"You sure did," said her mother. "And all by
yourself! I'm very proud of you!"

"I didn't know you could read THAT much," said Andrew. "Can I borrow your book?"

Megan laughed. "Sure," she said. "But it's not about dinosaurs!"

When everyone had gone, Megan's mother gave her a big, big hug. "You were wonderful!" she said. "You saved the day!"

"Yay!" said Megan. "Now I'll read every book in the whole library!"

And she started right away.

Story Hour – Starring Megan!

Meet the Author and Illustrator

Julie Brillhart used to work as a librarian before she began writing and illustrating children's books. Many of the ideas for her books came from working with children in the library. She takes everyday moments and turns them into stories and art.

Although her own children are grown, her favorite thing to do is to go to the children's room at her local library. Every week she spends an afternoon picking out children's books to take home and read.

Theme Connections

Think About It

Have you ever shared stories with younger children? Here are some questions to think about:

- What book would you share with the children in the library? Why would you pick that one?
- Would you pick the same story to share with your classmates? Why or why not?

Check the Concept/Question Board and answer any questions you can. Post any new questions you have.

Record Ideas

In your Writing Journal, tell what kind of story you like better—humorous or realistic fiction—and tell why.

Tell a Story

You will need three pieces of paper for your story. Draw a sad face on one paper, a light bulb on another paper, and a happy face on the third paper. Write a problem under the sad face. Write how to solve the problem under the light bulb. Write how the story ends under the happy face. Put the story in order: (1) sad face, (2) light bulb, (3) happy face. Share your story with classmates.

My Book!

David L. Harrison

illustrated by Anna Rich

I did it!
I did it!
Come and look
At what I've done!
I read a book!
When someone wrote it
Long ago
For me to read,
How did he know
That this was the book
I'd take from the shelf
And lie on the floor
And read by myself?

I really read it!
Just like that!
Word by word,
From first to last!
I'm sleeping with
This book in bed,
This first FIRST book
I've ever read!

Ant and the Three Little Figs

Betsy Byars
illustrated by Marc Simont

Ant said, "Read me a story."

I like to read.

I said, "Okay."

Ant sat down by me.

I opened the book

and began to read.

"Once upon a time

there were three little figs."

Ant sat up.

He said, "No! That is not right.

It's pigs. Three little PIGS.

Say PIGS."

I am easy to get along with.

I said, "Pigs."

The Ant leaned back.

He said, "Now read the story."

I read: "Once upon a time

there were three little bananas."

Ant said, "No! Don't do that!

Read the story right.

It's pigs.

Look at the picture.

There's a pig.

There's a pig.

There's a pig.

Three pigs!"

"Oh, all right. Pigs.

Once upon a time

there were three little—"

"Pigs," Ant said quickly.

"Who is reading this—

you or me?" I asked.

"You are," Ant said,

but you have to say pigs."

"And you have to let me read.

Once upon a time

there were three little—"

I stopped and waited.

The Ant waited, too.

Finally he said,

"This is your last chance.

If you don't say pigs, I'm leaving."

I said, "Oh, all right.

Once upon a time

there were three little pigs. . . ."

Ant got down from the chair.

I said, "Where are you going, Ant?

I read it right. I said pigs."

Ant said, "I am going outside."

"Why, Ant?"

"I don't like the rest of the story.

It has a big bad wolf in it."

I said, "I could change that, Ant.

I could make him a big bad lemon.

Or how about a big bad watermelon?"

"No," said Ant,

"I would know it was a wolf."

Ant went to the door and opened it.

He looked back at me.

He said, "But thank you

for reading to me."

"You are welcome, Ant,"

I said, "anytime."

Ant and the Three Little Figs

Meet the Author

Betsy Byars remembers her father changing certain parts of a story as he read it to her when she was young. This made her look closely at the written word. She always loved books, but she did not start writing books until her children were teenagers. She said, *"In that, writing is like baseball or piano playing. You have got to practice if you want to be successful."*

Meet the Illustrator

Marc Simont was born in Paris, France. Because his parents traveled a lot, he became very skillful at looking closely at the things around him. As a child he taught himself to draw by studying a picture book. He painted portraits and drew illustrations for advertisements before he became an illustrator for children's books. *"I believe that if I like the drawings I do, children will like them also,"* he said.

Theme Connections

Think About It

Here are some things to talk about:

- Have you ever shared a silly story with someone?
- Did you read it in a book or did you make it up yourself?
- What was the name of the silly story? What was it about?
- Has someone ever shared a silly story with you? What was it about?

Check the Concept/Question Board and answer any questions you can. Post new questions you have.

Record Ideas

In your Writing Journal, write some titles for *The Three Little Pigs* or another well-known story.

Finish the Story

Ant's big brother didn't finish the story. Finish a silly version for him.

- Write down what happens in the story *The Three Little Pigs*.
- Begin the story like Ant's big brother.
- Review what happens next and change some of the details to make the story silly.
- Share your silly story with classmates.

Books to the Ceiling

by Arnold Lobel

Books to the ceiling,
books to the sky.
My piles of books are
    a mile high.
How I love them!
How I need them!
I'll have a long beard by
    the time I read them.

Tomás and the Library Lady

Pat Mora

illustrated by Raul Colón

It was midnight. The light of the full moon followed the tired old car. Tomás was tired too. Hot and tired. He missed his own bed, in his own house in Texas.

   Tomás was on his way to Iowa again with
his family. His mother and father were farm
workers. They picked fruit and vegetables
for Texas farmers in the winter and for Iowa
farmers in the summer. Year after year they
bump-bumped along in their rusty old car.
"Mamá," whispered Tomás, "if I had a glass
of cold water, I would drink it in large gulps.
I would suck the ice. I would pour the last
drops of water on my face."

Tomás was glad when the car finally stopped. He helped his grandfather, Papá Grande, climb down. Tomás said, *"Buenas noches"*—"Good night"—to Papá, Mamá, Papá Grande, and to his little brother, Enrique. He curled up on the cot in the small house that his family shared with the other workers.

Early the next morning Mamá and Papá
went out to pick corn in the green fields. All
day they worked in the hot sun. Tomás and
Enrique carried water to them. Then the
boys played with a ball Mamá had sewn
from an old teddy bear.

When they got hot, they sat under a tree
with Papá Grande. "Tell us the story about
the man in the forest," said Tomás.

Tomás liked to listen to Papá Grande tell
stories in Spanish. Papá Grande was the best
storyteller in the family.

"En un tiempo pasado," Papá Grande began. "Once upon a time . . . on a windy night a man was riding a horse through a forest. The wind was howling, *whooooooooo*, and the leaves were blowing, *whish, whish* . . .

"All of a sudden something grabbed the man. He couldn't move. He was too scared to look around. All night long he wanted to ride away. But he couldn't.

"How the wind howled, *whooooooooo*. How the leaves blew. How his teeth chattered!

"Finally the sun came up. Slowly the man turned around. And who do you think was holding him?"

Tomás smiled and said, "A thorny tree."

Papá Grande laughed. "Tomás, you know all my stories," he said. "There are many more in the library. You are big enough to go by yourself. Then you can teach us new stories."

The next morning Tomás walked downtown. He looked at the big library. Its tall windows were like eyes glaring at him. Tomás walked around and around the big building. He saw children coming out carrying books. Slowly he started climbing up, up the steps. He counted them to himself in Spanish. *Uno, dos, tres, cuatro . . .* His mouth felt full of cotton.

Tomás stood in front of the library doors. He pressed his nose against the glass and peeked in. The library was huge!

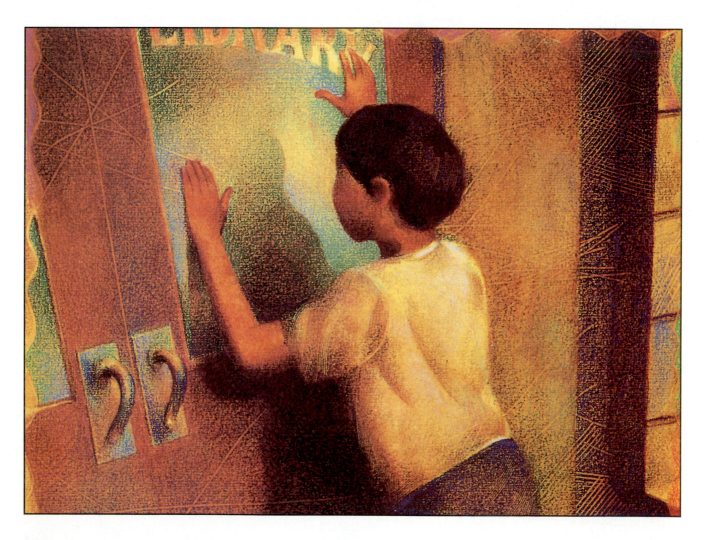

A hand tapped his shoulder. Tomás jumped.
A tall lady looked down at him. "It's a hot
day," she said. "Come inside and have a drink
of water. What's your name?" she asked.

"Tomás," he said.

"Come, Tomás," she said.

Inside it was cool. Tomás had never seen so many books. The lady watched him. "Come," she said again, leading him to a drinking fountain. "First some water. Then I will bring books to this table for you. What would you like to read about?"

"Tigers. Dinosaurs," said Tomás.

Tomás drank the cold water. He looked at the tall ceiling. He looked at all the books around the room. He watched the lady take some books from the shelves and bring them to the table. "This chair is for you, Tomás," she said. Tomás sat down. Then very carefully he took a book from the pile and opened it.

Tomás saw dinosaurs bending their long necks to lap shiny water. He heard the cries of a wild snakebird. He felt the warm neck of the dinosaur as he held on tight for a ride. Tomás forgot about the library lady. He forgot about Iowa and Texas.

"Tomás, Tomás," said the library lady
softly. Tomás looked around. The library
was empty. The sun was setting.

The library lady looked at Tomás for a
long time. She said, "Tomás, would you like
to borrow two library books? I will check
them out in my name."

Tomás walked out of the library carrying
his books. He ran home, eager to show the
new stories to his family.

Papá Grande looked at the library books. "Read to me," he said to Tomás. First Tomás showed him the pictures. He pointed to the tiger. "*¡Qué tigre tan grande!*" Tomás said first in Spanish and then in English, "What a big tiger!"

"Read to me in English," said Papá Grande. Tomás read about tiger eyes shining brightly in the jungle at night. He roared like a huge tiger. Papá, Mamá, and Enrique laughed. They came and sat near him to hear his story.

Some days Tomás went with his parents to the town dump. They looked for pieces of iron to sell. Enrique looked for toys. Tomás looked for books. He would put the books in the sun to bake away the smell.

All summer, whenever he could, Tomás went to the library. The library lady would say, "First a drink of water and then some new books, Tomás."

On quiet days the library lady said, "Come to my desk and read to me, Tomás." Then she would say, "Please teach me some new words in Spanish."

Tomás would smile. He liked being the teacher. The library lady pointed to a book. "Book is *libro*," said Tomás.

"*Libro*," said the library lady.

"*Pájaro*," said Tomás, flapping his arms.

The library lady laughed. "Bird," she said.

On days when the library was busy, Tomás read to himself. He'd look at the pictures for a long time. He smelled the smoke at an Indian camp. He rode a black horse across a hot, dusty desert.

And in the evenings he would read the stories to Mamá, Papá, Papá Grande, and Enrique.

One August afternoon Tomás brought Papá Grande to the library.

The library lady said, "*Buenas tardes, señor.*" Tomás smiled. He had taught the library lady how to say "Good afternoon, sir" in Spanish.

"*Buenas tardes, señora,*" Papá Grande replied.

Softly Tomás said, "I have a sad word to teach you today. The word is *adiós*. It means good-bye."

Tomás was going back to Texas. He would miss this quiet place, the cool water, the many books. He would miss the library lady.

"My mother sent this to thank you," said Tomás, handing her a small package. "It is *pan dulce*, sweet bread. My mother makes the best *pan dulce* in Texas."

The library lady said, "How nice. How very nice. *Gracias*, Tomás. Thank you." She gave Tomás a big hug.

That night, bumping along again in the
tired old car, Tomás held a shiny new book,
a present from the library lady. Papá Grande
smiled and said, "More stories for the new
storyteller."

84

Tomás closed his eyes. He saw the
dinosaurs drinking cool water long ago. He
heard the cry of the wild snakebird. He felt
the warm neck of the dinosaur as he held on
tight for a bumpy ride.

Tomás and the Library Lady

Meet the Author

Pat Mora's family spoke two languages at home, so she learned to speak and write in both English and Spanish. She was able to use both in her writing, as in "Tomás and the Library Lady." Pat Mora was a teacher for nearly twenty years before she began a career as a writer. She writes poetry and nonfiction, as well as children's literature. *"I've always enjoyed reading all kinds of books and now I get to write them too, to sit and play with words on my computer."*

Meet the Illustrator

Raul Colón dreamed of becoming an artist as a young child. He would hand in his homework with doodles and drawings. He likes to scratch the paper with a special tool before he uses colored pencils. This gives his illustrations a special effect. His work has included puppet designs, album covers, short animated films, and illustrations for children's books.

Theme Connections

Think About It

Tomás's family often shared stories. Does your family ever tell or read stories to each other? Here are some questions to discuss:

- Who shares stories in your family?
- What sorts of stories do they tell or read?
- When do people in your family tell or read stories to each other?

Check the Concept/Question Board and answer any questions you can. Post any new questions you have.

Record Ideas

 In your Writing Journal, record the names of stories that your family reads or shares with you. Print two or three sentences about the stories.

Share a Story

You may know a story well because you have heard a story many times.

- Share a favorite story you know well.
- Tell the story in your own words to a group of classmates.
- You may change your voice when different characters speak.

FINE Art

The Library. 1960. **Jacob Lawrence.** Tempera on fiberboard.
60.9 × 75.8 cm. Gift of S.C. Johnson & Son, Inc. The National
Museum of American Art. Photo: Art Resource, NY.

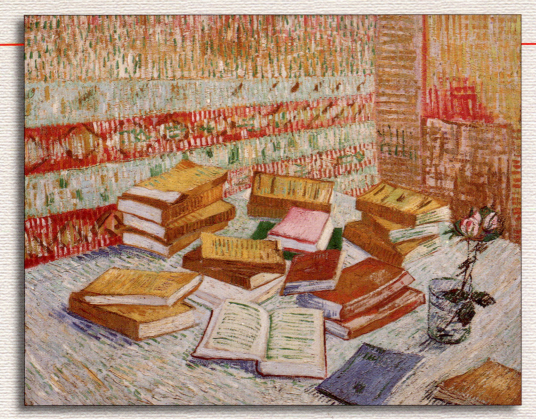

Jungle Tales. 1895. **James J. Shannon.** Oil on canvas. 87 × 113.7 cm. The Metropolitan Museum of Art, Arthur Hoppock Hearn Fund, 1913. Photograph © 1988 The Metropolitan Museum of Art.

89

Sequoyah

Inventor of the Cherokee Written Language

Diane Shaughnessy and Jack Carpenter
illustrated by Sandy Rabinowitz

Sequoyah's mother was a Cherokee woman named Wureth. His father was a white man named Nathaniel Gist.

Sequoyah

Sequoyah was born around 1770 in the village of Tuskegee in what is now the state of Alabama. Most Americans knew Sequoyah as George Guess, but the Cherokees called him Sogwali. British **missionaries** gave him the name Sequoyah.

The Cherokees once lived in the area that is now the states of North Carolina, South Carolina, Tennessee, Georgia, and Alabama. Today, they live in the state of Oklahoma.

Sequoyah was raised as a Cherokee. He is famous for inventing the **syllabary** for the Cherokee language. The syllabary is an alphabet whose letters stand for the **syllables** that make up the words in the Cherokee language. Sequoyah created a way for the Cherokees to write in their own language.

The Cherokee Nation

The Cherokee Indians once lived in the southern part of the Appalachian Mountains. This area is now the states of North Carolina, South Carolina, Tennessee, Georgia, and Alabama. Today, they live in what is now the state of Oklahoma.

The Cherokees were forced by the U.S. government to leave their homeland in the Appalachian Mountains.

The Cherokees called themselves Ani-Yunwiya. They were given the name "Cherokee" by a tribe who lived nearby. Cherokee means "people of a different language." The Cherokee Nation was strong and powerful. They were leaders among the Native Americans in their area.

A Man of Words

As a young man, Sequoyah was a brave **warrior** and a good hunter and **trader**. He also worked as a **silversmith**. He was able to speak many languages, including Cherokee, Spanish, and French. This made him a good **interpreter** between the Cherokees and the neighboring white settlers.

Like many young Cherokee men, Sequoyah was a good hunter. He was also good at learning new languages.

Sequoyah was interested in the way white people could **communicate** with each other by writing on sheets of paper. Some Native Americans called this "talking leaves."

Keeping the Language

Sequoyah saw young Cherokees learning English to communicate with white people. He was afraid that these Cherokees would forget their own language and **culture**. People use language to preserve their cultural **traditions** and history.

Sequoyah was afraid that without a written language the Cherokees would lose their culture to the white settlers.

96

At that time, Cherokee was only a spoken language. There were no letters that Cherokee people could use to make words to write with. Sequoyah believed that he could create a written form of the Cherokee language. In that way, the Cherokee culture could be kept alive.

Getting to Work

In 1809, Sequoyah began to work on creating a Cherokee alphabet. At first, Sequoyah drew a picture for each Cherokee word or idea. He soon realized that it would take too many pictures to write down one sentence. No one would be able to learn or remember that many pictures.

During this time, Sequoyah built himself a cabin in the woods, away from his wife and family. He needed time alone to work. His friends couldn't understand why he was spending so much time on this project.

Sequoyah lived by himself in a small cabin like this in the woods while he worked. He once said that trying to write sounds down on paper was "like catching a wild beast and taming it."

Starting Over

Sequoyah's wife finally became tired of Sequoyah's project. One night, she went to his cabin and threw all of his papers into the fireplace. Some people would have been angry. But Sequoyah saw this as a new beginning. He started the work all over again.

This time, instead of breaking sentences into words, Sequoyah broke the words into sounds, or syllables. He drew one **character** for each syllable. He knew that all Cherokee words were made up of the same sounds. The sounds, or syllables, were put together in different ways to make words.

Cherokee Alphabet

These are the symbols that Sequoyah created for each syllable.

Cherokee Talking Leaves

Twelve years later, in 1821, Sequoyah had developed 86 characters. This was later changed to 85. Sequoyah took his syllabary, or alphabet based on syllables, to the leaders of the Cherokee Nation. They were amazed.

They quickly accepted Sequoyah's characters as the Cherokee written language. The Cherokees finally had their own "talking leaves." They were the first Native Americans to develop a written language.

Most Cherokee people find it easy to learn and use Sequoyah's syllabary. This is what the words "boy" and "girl" look like in Cherokee.

Using the Language

In 1822, Sequoyah visited Cherokees who lived in other areas. He taught them to read and write the new language. Soon most Cherokees could read and write Cherokee.

In 1827, the Cherokee tribal leaders wrote their own **constitution** using their new written language. The leaders also agreed to set aside money for a Cherokee newspaper. One year later, the first edition of the *Cherokee Phoenix* was printed. The articles were printed in English and Cherokee.

The *Cherokee Phoenix* was the first Native American newspaper ever published in the United States.

The Trail of Tears

In 1838 and 1839, the U.S. government decided it wanted the Cherokee land for white settlers. Soldiers forced the Cherokee people to move nearly 900 miles west of their homeland, to what is now the state of Oklahoma. This forced march was later called the "Trail of Tears."

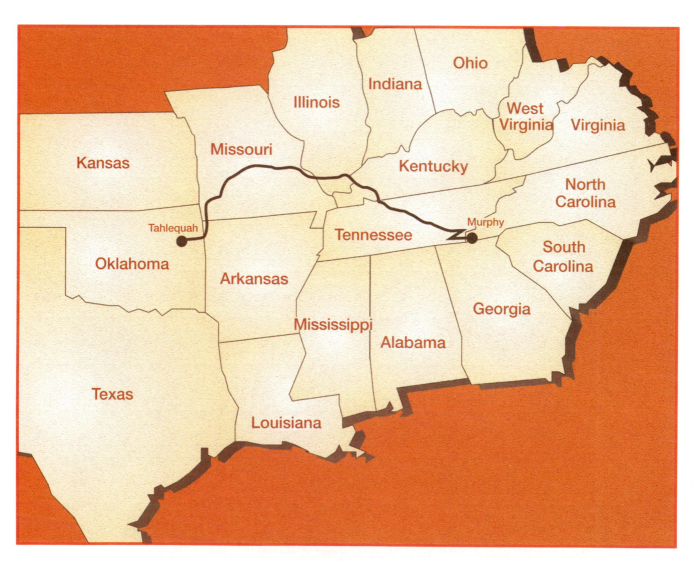

The Cherokees who survived the long march from their homeland to Oklahoma called the march "The Place Where They Cried." Today, it is called the Trail of Tears.

Of the 16,000 people who walked the Trail of Tears, over 4,000 people died. It is not known whether Sequoyah made the march. But he did move to Oklahoma around that time. Sequoyah lived to be 84. He died in 1843.

A Strong Nation

The Cherokee written language is believed to be the only known language created by one person and used by many. To honor Sequoyah, the giant sequoia trees found in California's Yosemite Valley were named for him. Thanks to Sequoyah's characters, nearly everyone in the Cherokee Nation can read and write in Cherokee.

Today, the Cherokee Nation is still one of the strongest Native American nations in the United States. They have a written history that can be passed down from parent to child, and will never be forgotten.

Sequoyah

Inventor of the Cherokee Written Language

Meet the Authors

Diane Shaughnessy lives in Tampa, Florida with her two cats named Sugar and Spice. She enjoys creating and collecting pottery. Many of her writings and art works have Native American themes.

    Jack Carpenter's interest in Native Americans started when he was doing research about his own family's history. Through his research he had the opportunity to write several biographies about important Native Americans. He also writes music and poetry. He said, *"The children's books, the music, and the poetry I write as a pleasurable hobby. Not as a living. I do these things for fun."*

Meet the Illustrator

Sandy Rabinowitz was surrounded by art when she was growing up. Both her parents taught art, and the classes were often held in their home. As an adult, her first published work was a story of her father's she retold and illustrated, called *The Red Horse and the Bluebird.*

    Sandy said, *"I was pleased to have been chosen to illustrate "Sequoyah" because I enjoy illustrating historical stories that require rustic backgrounds and earthy colors."*

Theme Connections

Think About It

Did Sequoyah help the Cherokee share their stories? How? Here is a question to think about:

- What might happen to the stories of the Cherokee people if Sequoyah had not invented a way to write their language?

Check the Concept/Question Board and answer any questions you can. Post any new questions you have.

Record Ideas

Who has written the stories you share with your classmates? List your favorite authors. Then, write the books you like best.

Write a Book Review

A book review is a short paragraph that shares facts and your feelings about a story. Write a book review for the life story of Sequoyah you read.

- Jot down some ideas about the story. Did you like it? Why or why not? What happens in this story? What did you learn from the story? Is this story like any other books you have read?
- Write a paragraph about the book. Use your notes to get started.
- Share your book review with classmates.

The Pen

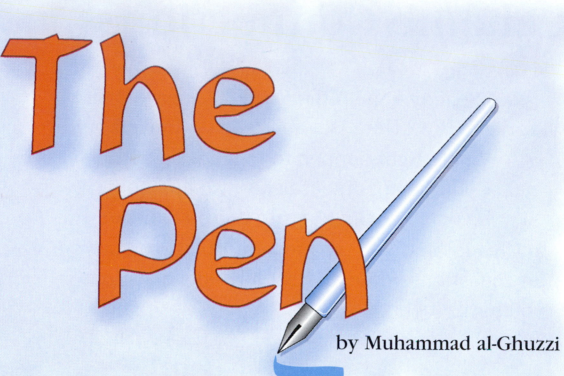

by Muhammad al-Ghuzzi

Take a pen in your uncertain fingers.
Trust, and be assured
That the whole world is a sky-blue butterfly,
and that words are the nets to capture it.

A Word Is Dead

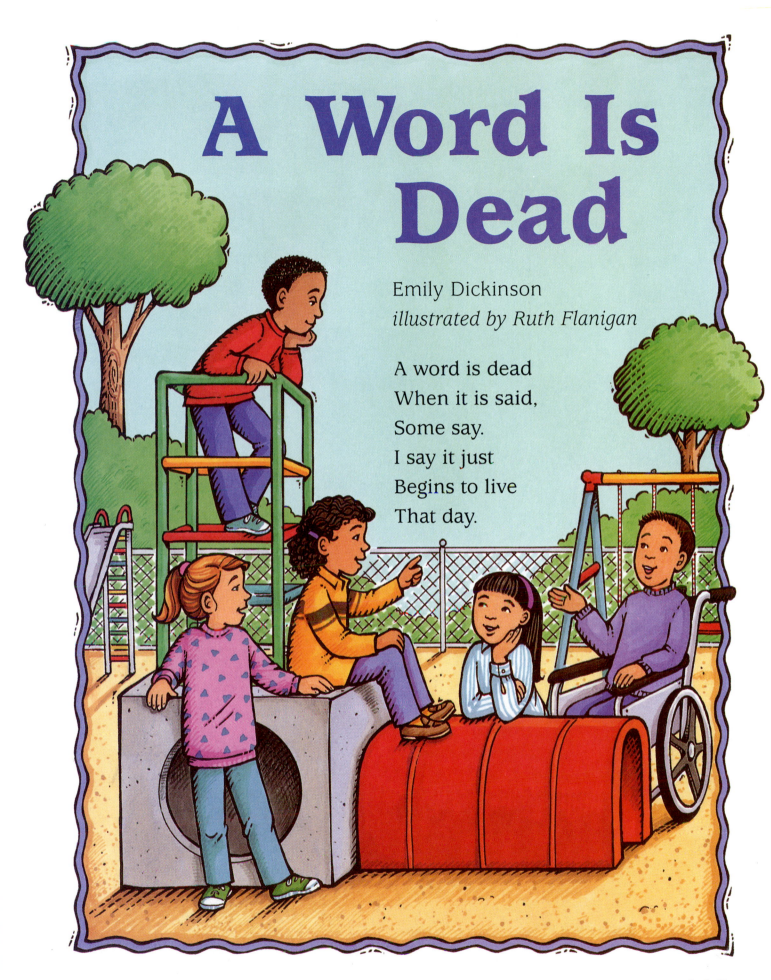

Emily Dickinson
illustrated by Ruth Flanigan

A word is dead
When it is said,
Some say.
I say it just
Begins to live
That day.

Amber
on the Mountain

Tony Johnston
illustrated by Robert Duncan

Amber lived on a mountain so high, it poked through the clouds like a needle stuck in down. Trees bristled on it like porcupine quills. And the air made you giddy—it was that clear. Still, for all that soaring beauty, Amber was lonesome. For mountain people lived scattered far from one another.

Once a man came on horseback to teach the people to read and write. How Amber longed to read and write! Books would be good company. But mountain life was too hard for the man. He left his supplies behind and skedaddled before winter came.

One day another man came with a crew to build a road. His wife and daughter, Anna, came too.

Amber's Granny Cotton told the man straight out, "You can't build a road here. Folks will roll clean off it, like walking up a wall."

But the man said, "You can do almost anything you fix your mind on."

He fixed his mind on building that road.

Now Amber had seen Anna with her family, inching their way up the mountain. She wanted to be friends.

But Amber was shy.

I will say "hey" to her when the time is right, Amber thought.

Meanwhile, she watched Anna, biding her time.

One day Amber was watching. Anna lay flopped on her stomach in a meadow, reading a book. The sky was streaked with morning. The air was warm. The grass hummed with bees.

Suddenly, up jumped Anna shouting, *"Once upon a time—"* and hopping around, crazy as a doodlebug.

Amber decided the time was right to say "hey."

"Hey!" she called. "Are you crazy?"

"Sure!" Anna called back. "Crazy with spring! Hey, yourself!"

"What are you shouting?" asked Amber.

"A story from my book. About a princess spinning gold."

"Might I hold it?" Amber asked.

"Sure."

Amber took the book as if it were a fine and breakable cup. She examined the pages.

"This tells of a princess—truly?" she asked.

"Yep. Want to read it?"

"I don't know how," Amber said. "There's no school hereabouts."

"I forgot," said Anna.

She stared at Amber. A stubborn look came into her eyes.

Amber giggled. "You look like our mule, Rockhead. When old Rockhead looks balkity, he's up to something sure."

"Well, I *am* up to something," said Anna. "Daddy says you can do almost anything you fix your mind on. I've just fixed mine on teaching you to read!"

"For real and true?" cried Amber.

"For real and true."

Anna began shouting from the book again. Amber joined in. Then they twirled through the grass, crazy as *two* doodlebugs.

After that, Anna and Amber stuck to each other like burrs.

When Amber did her chores, Anna helped. She learned to slop the pigs, milk the goat, and gather eggs. When Granny Cotton needed "young eyes" to help with her quilting, the girls sat on either side of her, poking little silver needles in and out, in and out.

Whatever else they did, every day they practiced reading.

Learning to read was like walking up a wall. Amber kept rolling off.

"These marks are like the chicken tracks in our yard," she moaned. "I know for a fact chickens don't write notes to each other. Are you certain sure these letters mean something?"

"Certain sure." Anna smiled.

Sometimes Amber read a few words. Then she stumbled. Sometimes she forgot the words and had to start all over. She was so eager, she hurried and tangled the words like quilting thread.

"Drat!" Amber grumbled. "I plain can't do this!"

127

"You *can*," said Anna. "Just pretend you're old Rockhead. Set your whole self to the task."

Amber stiffened up mulish as could be.

Anna howled with delight. "Now *that* is the face of a reader!"

And one day—one very fine day— Amber took the book and read, "And he stamped his foot through the floor and was never seen again. The end."

"You did it!" hooted Anna. "You read all by yourself!"

"I read! I read! I READ!"

The girls marched around, stomping their feet like Rumpelstiltskin.

Suddenly Anna stopped. She stared at Amber.

"Just what notion have you *now*, Miss Rockhead?" Amber asked.

"Now I've fixed my mind on teaching you to write!" said Anna.

But that was not to be. The road was finished. Anna and her family were going home.

When the day of parting came, each gave the other a gift. Anna gave Amber her book of fairy tales. Amber gave Anna a little clay mule.

Then Amber watched her friend down the mountain till she melted into blue mountain mist.

Months passed. Mountain people went down the road and learned the ease of city ways. City people came up the road and learned the beauty of mountain ways. And funny thing—not one solitary soul rolled off that road.

From time to time up on the mountain, Amber got a letter from Anna. Then she glowed with happiness. Anna's words set them side by side again. But Amber was sad too. She missed her friend. And she could not tell her so.

But one day she got a notion. A wonderful, rockheaded notion.

"Attention! Attention!" she announced to the chickens. "I've fixed my mind on learning to write. Soon I'll send Anna a letter frilly as lace. And she'll faint right to the floor!"

The chickens paid no attention. Amber didn't care. She ran straight to Granny Cotton, jibbering her news out before she stopped.

Granny chuckled. "Child, child, you're peltering me with words, thick as spring rain. I feel drenched."

Granny was so pleased, she gave Amber the paper and pencils left behind by the teacher long ago.

Whenever she could squeeze in time, Amber took her book and tried to copy the words.

If I can read 'em, I can copy 'em, she thought.

At first they looked squat and squashed.

"My letters are lopsided as a herd of one-horned cows," she groaned.

Amber kept working.

When it snowed and the world outside was muffled in white, she huddled under a quilt so only her hands poked out. Cold and stiff, she formed her letters.

When clouds like grey geese flocked in the sky and rain glazed the land, Amber shivered. But she kept working.

Her tongue curled to her upper lip in concentration, like a lizard stalking a bug. She squeezed her pencil nearly to splinters. Her fingers hurt. Still, she kept working.

And one day—one very fine day—Amber sent a letter to Anna.

Dear Anna,

I am a rockhead to. I fixed my mind on riting. I teached myself to rite sos I can rite you. I hop you faynt to the flor.

Love from yer frend Amber

Soon a letter came back.

Dear Rockhead,

Your letter made me faint right <u>through</u> the floor, like you-know-who! It made me happy. You are not far away anymore.

Love from your friend,

Anna

Amber on the Mountain

Meet the Author

Tony Johnston loved reading books as a child. Her interest in writing was *"partly a desire to be in that other world of fantasy."* Her main characters—both human and animal—are often quirky. The setting of her stories is important to her. She lived in Mexico for several years and this became the setting of several of her books. She said, *"My goal in writing is simply to entertain—myself and someone else."*

Meet the Illustrator

Robert Duncan was born in Utah. He was eleven years old when he began painting. After studying art at the University of Utah, he worked as a commercial artist. Now he devotes all of his time to art of the American West. *"I enjoy using painting as a vehicle to celebrate my family and joys of a simple life."* His work can be found in galleries and on posters, prints, and cards. "Amber on the Mountain" is his first book.

Theme Connections

Think About It

"Amber on the Mountain" shows how learning to read and write can help us share stories. Here are some things to talk about:

- What did the story tell you about sharing?
- Were you able to share more stories once you could read?
- If you had a friend like Amber, what stories would you share with her?

Check the Concept/Question Board and answer any questions you can.

Record Ideas

 In your Writing Journal, record your thoughts about how reading and writing can help you share stories.

Write a Letter

Write a letter to someone who lives far away.

- You may want to tell about what you are learning in school.
- You may want to list some stories you enjoy.
- You may want to ask some questions.
- Draft your letter. You may start by writing about some ideas listed above.
- Proofread your letter and make a final copy.

Bibliography

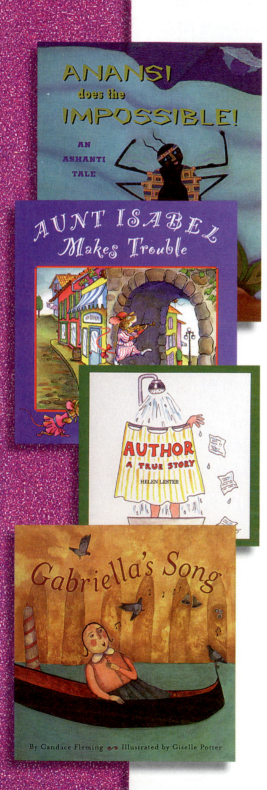

Anansi does the Impossible

by Verna Aardema. Where do stories come from? A spider and his wife? Impossible? Read and find out.

Aunt Isabel Makes Trouble

by Kate Duke. Have you ever wanted a story to go on forever? So does Penelope.

Author: A True Story

by Helen Lester. How do you become a writer? This writer started at three years old. Share her story.

Gabriella's Song

by Candace Fleming. Come to Venice where Gabriella's story is set to music. Read about songs, melodies, and memories.

Keepers

by Jeri Hanel Watts. Kenyon catches more than balls with his new baseball glove; he catches on. What's the story and who will be the story keeper?

More Than Anything Else

by Marie Bradby. Meet nine-year-old Booker T. Washington and see why he wants to learn to read more than anything else. Why is it so important to him? Is it important to you?

Sarah's Story

by Bill Harley. What happens to Sarah on the way to school? Whatever it is, it gives her the best story ever to tell her class.

Too Much Talk

by Angela Shelf Medearis. What happens when yams and fish and dogs start talking? Read this West African folktale and find out just how much talk is too much.

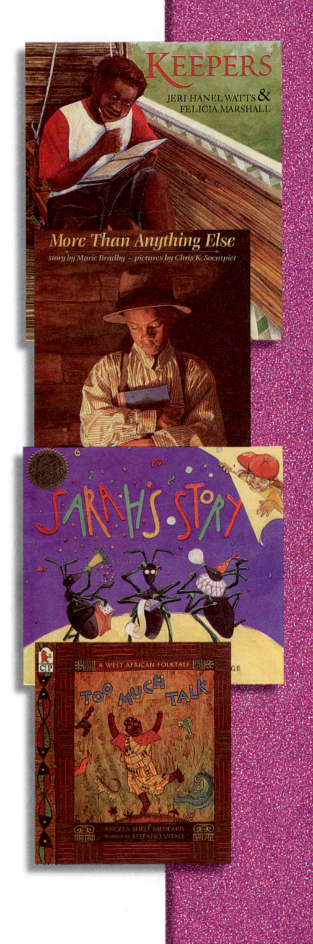

Kindness

What does it mean to be kind? Who is kind? How do you know? Stories can help us learn about kindness.

Mushroom in the Rain

retold by Mirra Ginsburg

illustrated by José Aruego and Ariane Dewey

One day an ant was caught in the rain. "Where can I hide?" he wondered.

He saw a tiny mushroom peeking out of the ground in a clearing, and he hid under it. He sat there, waiting for the rain to stop. But the rain came down harder and harder.

A wet butterfly crawled up to the mushroom.

"Cousin Ant, let me come in from the rain. I am so wet I cannot fly."

"How can I let you in?" said the ant. "There is barely room enough for one."

"It does not matter," said the butterfly. "Better crowded than wet."

The ant moved over and made room for the butterfly. The rain came down harder and harder.

A mouse ran up.

"Let me in under the mushroom. I am drenched to the bone."

"How can we let you in? There is no more room here."

"Just move a little closer!"

They huddled closer and let the mouse in. And the rain came down and came down and would not stop.

A little sparrow hopped up to the
mushroom, crying: "My feathers are
dripping, my wings are so tired! Let me in
under the mushroom to dry out and rest
until the rain stops!"

"But there is no room here."

"Please! Move over just a little!"

They moved over, and there was room
enough for the sparrow.

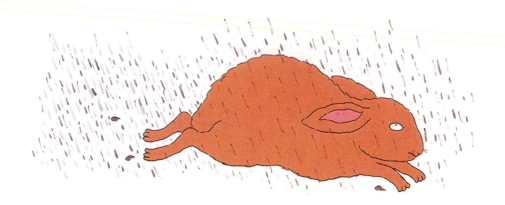

Then a rabbit hopped into the clearing and saw the mushroom.

"Oh, hide me!" he cried. "Save me! A fox is chasing me!"

"Poor rabbit," said the ant. "Let's crowd ourselves a little more and take him in."

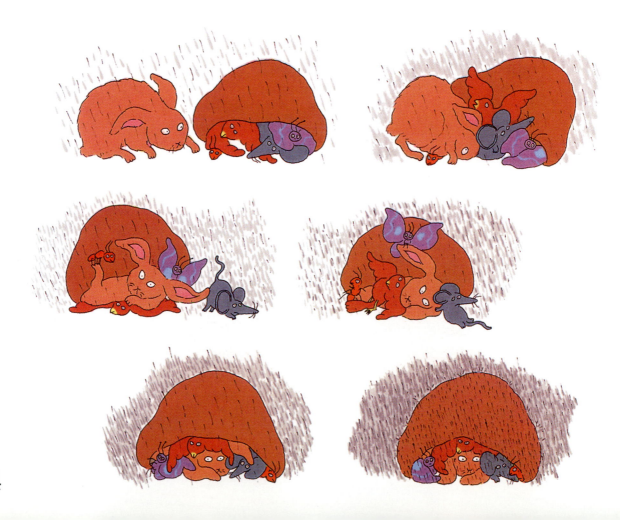

As soon as they hid the rabbit, the fox
came running.

"Have you seen the rabbit? Which way did
he go?" he asked.

"We have not seen him."

The fox came nearer and sniffed. "There is
a rabbit smell around. Isn't he hiding here?"

"You silly fox! How could a rabbit get in here? Don't you see there isn't any room?"

The fox turned up his nose, flicked his tail, and ran off.

By then the rain was over. The sun looked out from behind the clouds. And everyone came out from under the mushroom, bright and merry.

The ant looked at his neighbors. "How could this be? At first I had hardly room enough under the mushroom just for myself, and in the end all five of us were able to sit under it."

"Qua-ha-ha! Qua-ha-ha!" somebody laughed loudly behind them.

They turned and saw a fat green frog sitting on top of the mushroom, shaking his head at them.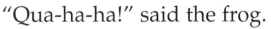

"Qua-ha-ha!" said the frog. "Don't you know what happens to a mushroom in the rain?" And he hopped away, still laughing.

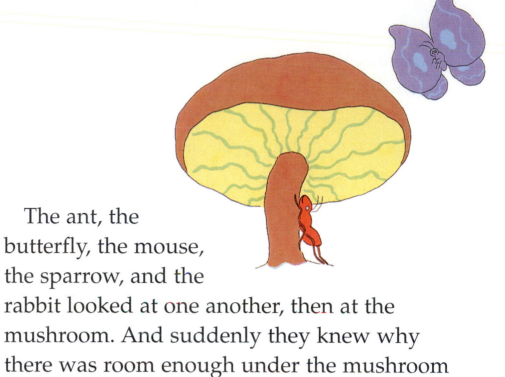

The ant, the
butterfly, the mouse,
the sparrow, and the
rabbit looked at one another, then at the
mushroom. And suddenly they knew why
there was room enough under the mushroom
for them all.

Do you know? Can you guess what
happens to a mushroom when it rains?

IT GROWS!

Mushroom in the Rain

Meet the Author

Mirra Ginsburg was born in a small Russian village much like the towns in the folktales that she loved to read. She began writing children's books by taking books written in Russian or Yiddish and rewriting them in English so that American children could enjoy them. Before long, she was making up her own stories. She said, *"From my father, I learned to love animals and green growing things. As a child, I was surrounded with them."*

Meet the Illustrators

José Aruego and Ariane Dewey have combined their talents and have illustrated more than sixty children's books. Mr. Aruego does the drawings and Ms. Dewey adds the color through paint. José Aruego began a career in law, but after a few months he realized that he wanted to draw, not practice law. After graduating from art school, he began drawing cartoons and later began illustrating children's books. Ariane Dewey always loved bright colors. In fourth grade art class, she painted bright pink kids swimming in a blue-green lake. Her love of joyful colors is seen in many children's books.

Theme Connections

Think About It

Although "Mushroom in the Rain" is a fantasy, people sometimes act the same way as the characters in this story.

- Were the story characters always kind to each other? Why or why not?
- Which animal were they kindest to? Why?
- Which animal were they meanest to? Why?
- Do you think Ant was kind? Why or why not?

If you have any questions about Kindness, post them on the Concept/Question Board.

Record Ideas

What have you learned about kindness from this story? Record your thoughts in your Writing Journal.

Write a Paragraph

Pick one of the story characters and imagine how he or she looked in the rain.

- Write about how he or she looks, and how that makes you feel.
- Tell why you felt that way. Can you think of more than one reason?
- Tell how it would make you feel if you were the story character.
- Draw a picture of the character.

The Elves and the Shoemaker

retold by Freya Littledale

illustrated by Brinton Turkle

There was once a good shoemaker who became very poor. At last he had only one piece of leather to make one pair of shoes. "Well," said the shoemaker to his wife, "I will cut the leather tonight and make the shoes in the morning."

The next morning he went to his table, and he couldn't believe what he saw. The leather was polished. The sewing was done. And there was a fine pair of shoes! Not one stitch was out of place.

"Do you see what I see?" asked the shoemaker.

"Indeed I do," said his wife. "I see a fine pair of shoes."

"But who could have made them?" the shoemaker said.

"It's just like magic!" said his wife.

At that very moment a man came in with a top hat and cane. "Those shoes look right for me," said the man. And so they were. They were right from heel to toe. "How much do they cost?"

"One gold coin," said the shoemaker.

"I'll give you two," said the man.

And he went on his way with a smile on his face and the new shoes on his feet.

"Well, well," said the shoemaker, "now I can buy leather for two pairs of shoes." And he cut the leather that night so he could make the shoes in the morning.

The next morning the shoemaker woke up, and he found two pairs of ladies' shoes. They were shining in the sunlight.

"Who is making these shoes?" said the shoemaker. "They are the best shoes in the world."

167

At that very moment two ladies came in.
They looked exactly alike. "My, what pretty
shoes!" said the ladies. "They will surely fit
us." And the ladies were right. They gave the
shoemaker four gold coins and away they
went . . . clickety-clack, clickety-clack in
their pretty new shoes.

And so it went. Every night the shoemaker cut the leather. Every morning the shoes were made. And every day more people came to buy his beautiful shoes.

Just before Christmas the shoemaker said, "Whoever is making these shoes is making us very happy."

"And rich," said his wife.

"Let us stay up and see who it is," the shoemaker said.

"Good," said his wife. So they hid behind some coats, and they waited and waited and waited. When the clock struck twelve, in came two little elves.

"*Elves,*" cried the shoemaker.

"Shh!" said his wife.

At once the elves hopped up on the table and set to work. Tap-tap went their hammers. Snip-snap went their scissors. Stitch-stitch went their needles. Their tiny fingers moved so fast the shoemaker and his wife could hardly believe their eyes.

The elves sewed and they hammered and they didn't stop until all the shoes were finished. There were little shoes and big ones. There were white ones and black ones and brown ones. The elves lined them all in a row. Then they jumped down from the table. They ran across the room and out the door.

The next morning the wife said, "The elves have made us very happy. I want to make them happy too. They need new clothes to keep warm. So I'll make them pants and shirts and coats. And I'll knit them socks and hats. You can make them each a pair of shoes."

"Yes, yes!" said the shoemaker. And they went right to work.

On Christmas Eve the shoemaker left no leather on the table. He left all the pretty gifts instead. Then he and his wife hid behind the coats to see what the elves would do.

When the clock struck twelve, in came the elves, ready to set to work. But when they looked at the table and saw the fine clothes, they laughed and clapped their hands.

"How happy they are!" said the shoemaker's wife.

"Shhh," said her husband.

174

The elves put on the clothes, looked in the mirror, and began to sing:

What fine and handsome elves are we,
No longer cobblers will we be,
From now on we'll dance and play,
Into the woods and far away.

They hopped over the table and jumped over
the chairs. They skipped all around the room,
danced out the door, and were never seen again.
   But from that night on everything always went
well for the good shoemaker and his wife.

The Elves and the Shoemaker

Meet the Author

Freya Littledale spent much of her free time as a child reading. She especially enjoyed fairy tales. When she was nine-years old, she began writing her own stories and poems. She always loved writing and retelling stories for children. Littledale kept sharing her stories for the rest of her life.

Meet the Illustrator

Brinton Turkle has added his special magic to more than fifty children's books. *"I find the combination of words and pictures that is possible today only in children's books very exciting . . . children [who] must never be offered less than the very best."*

Theme Connections

Think About It

A kind act is returned in "The Elves and the Shoemaker." Here are some things to think about:

- Who are the kindest people in this story?
- Do you think the elves expected the shoemaker to return their kindness? Why?
- What does the story teach us about kindness?

Check the Concept/Question Board and answer any questions you can. Post any new questions you have about kindness.

Record Ideas

In your Writing Journal, record some ways in which the elves and the shoemaker showed kindness. Write some thoughts about how the elves and the shoemaker are the same and different.

Make a Chart

Make a chart showing the ways the elves and the shoemaker are the same and different. Here is one way to do it.

	Same	**Different**
Elves		
Shoemaker and His Wife		

The Paper Crane

by Molly Bang

A man once owned a restaurant on a busy road. He loved to cook good food and he loved to serve it. He worked from morning until night, and he was happy.

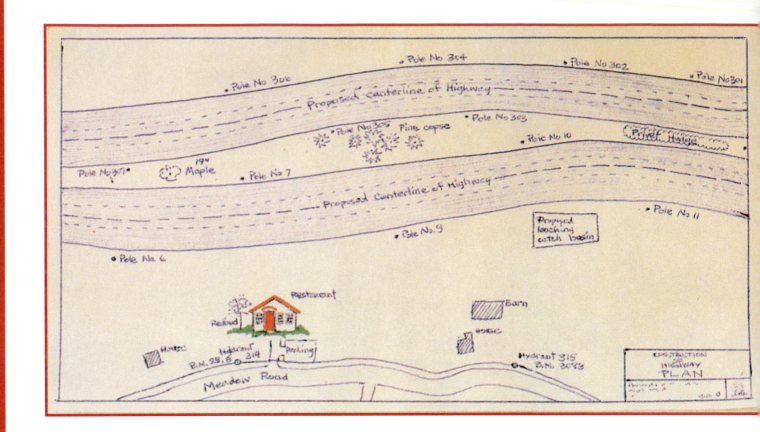

But a new highway was built close by.
Travelers drove straight from one place to
another and no longer stopped at the
restaurant. Many days went by when no
guests came at all. The man became very
poor, and had nothing to do but dust and
polish his empty plates and tables.

183

One evening a stranger came into the
restaurant. His clothes were old and worn,
but he had an unusual, gentle manner.

Though he said he had no money to pay
for food, the owner invited him to sit down.
He cooked the best meal he could make and
served him like a king.

When the stranger had finished, he said to his host, "I cannot pay you with money, but I would like to thank you in my own way."

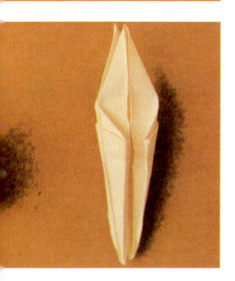

He picked up a paper napkin from the table and folded it into the shape of a crane. "You have only to clap your hands," he said, "and this bird will come to life and dance for you. Take it, and enjoy it while it is with you."

With these words the stranger left.

It happened just as the stranger had said.
The owner had only to clap his hands and
the paper crane became a living bird, flew
down to the floor, and danced.

188

Soon word of the dancing crane spread,
and people came from far and near to see the
magic bird perform.

The owner was happy again, for his
restaurant was always full of guests.

He cooked and served and had company
from morning until night.

The weeks passed.

And the months.

One evening a man came into the
restaurant. His clothes were old and worn,
but he had an unusual, gentle manner. The
owner knew him at once and was overjoyed.

The stranger, however, said nothing. He took a flute from his pocket, raised it to his lips, and began to play.

The crane flew down from its place on the shelf and danced as it had never danced before.

The stranger finished playing, lowered the flute from his lips, and returned it to his pocket. He climbed on the back of the crane, and they flew out of the door and away.

The restaurant still stands by the side of the road, and guests still come to eat the good food and hear the story of the gentle stranger and the magic crane made from a paper napkin. But neither the stranger nor the dancing crane has ever been seen again.

The Paper Crane

Meet the Author and Illustrator

Molly Bang's love of books began early. Her parents often gave each other books for birthdays and other holidays. After graduating from Wellesley College, she went to Japan to teach English.

Through her travels in other countries she has gathered many ideas for her books. In her writings she likes to blend Asian folktale themes with modern settings. Her illustrations show a real understanding of the people and places she writes about. She has even illustrated books for her mother, who is also an author.

196

Theme Connections

Think About It

"The Paper Crane" and "The Elves and the Shoemaker" are the same in some ways. How are they the same? Here are some things to think about:

- Do the shoemaker and the restaurant owner have the same kind of problem? What is it?
- Do the shoemaker's wife and the old man act the same way? What do they do the same?
- What did you learn about kindness from this story?

Check the Concept/Question Board and answer any questions that you can. Post any new questions you have about Kindness.

Record Ideas

 Write a brief description in your Writing Journal of how one of the characters showed kindness. Explain how that character felt.

Make a Character Comic Strip

You can illustrate how characters felt and acted in a comic strip.

- Draw four boxes in a row.
- Pick a character's kind act.
- Draw a picture in each box that shows how the kind act was done.
- Be sure to show how the characters felt.

FINE Art

The Good Samaritan. 1618–1622. **Domenico Fetti.** Oil on wood. 60 × 43.2 cm. The Metropolitan Museum of Art, Rogers Fund, 1930. Photograph ©1979 The Metropolitan Museum of Art.

***General and Horse
from the Tomb of
Emperor Tang
Taizong.*** 7th century.
Stone relief. University
of Pennsylvania Museum.
neg # T4-171c.

Susan Comforting the Baby. 1881. **Mary Cassatt.** Oil on
canvas. The Museum of Fine Arts, Houston; The John A. and
Audrey Jones Beck Collection.

Corduroy

by Don Freeman

Corduroy is a bear who once lived in the toy department of a big store. Day after day he waited with all the other animals and dolls for someone to come along and take him home.

The store was always filled with shoppers buying all sorts of things, but no one ever seemed to want a small bear in green overalls.

Then one morning a little girl stopped and looked straight into Corduroy's bright eyes.

"Oh, Mommy!" she said. "Look! There's the very bear I've always wanted."

"Not today, dear." Her mother sighed. "I've spent too much already. Besides, he doesn't look new. He's lost the button to one of his shoulder straps."

Corduroy watched them sadly as they walked away.

"I didn't know I'd lost a button," he said to himself. "Tonight I'll go and see if I can find it."

Late that evening, when all the shoppers had gone and the doors were shut and locked, Corduroy climbed carefully down from his shelf and began searching everywhere on the floor for his lost button.

Suddenly he felt the floor moving under him! Quite by accident he had stepped onto an escalator—and up he went!

"Could this be a mountain?" he wondered. "I think I've always wanted to climb a mountain."

He stepped off the escalator as it reached the next floor, and there, before his eyes, was a most amazing sight— tables and chairs and lamps and sofas, and rows and rows of beds. "This must be a palace!" Corduroy gasped. "I guess I've always wanted to live in a palace."

He wandered around admiring the furniture.

"This must be a bed," he said. "I've always wanted to sleep in a bed." And up he crawled onto a large, thick mattress.

All at once he saw something small and round.

"Why, here's my button!" he cried.
And he tried to pick it up. But, like all the
other buttons on the mattress, it was tied
down tight.

He yanked and pulled with both paws
until POP! Off came the button—and off
the mattress Corduroy toppled, *bang* into a
tall floor lamp. Over it fell with a crash!

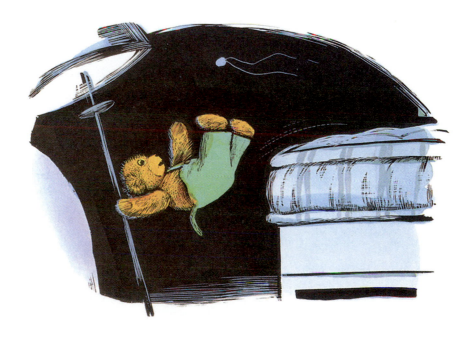

Corduroy didn't know it, but there was someone else awake in the store. The night watchman was going his rounds on the floor above. When he heard the crash he came dashing down the escalator.

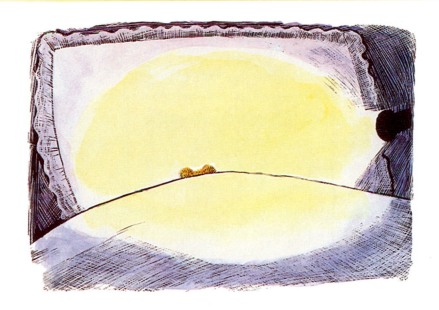

"Now who in the world did that!" he exclaimed. "Somebody must be hiding around here!"

He flashed his light under and over sofas and beds until he came to the biggest bed of all. And there he saw two fuzzy brown ears sticking up from under the cover.

"Hello!" he said. "How did *you* get upstairs?"

The watchman tucked Corduroy under his arm and carried him down the escalator and set him on the shelf in the toy department with the other animals and dolls.

Corduroy was just waking up when the first customers came into the store in the morning. And there, looking at him with a wide, warm smile, was the same little girl he'd seen only the day before.

"I'm Lisa," she said, "and you're going to be my very own bear. Last night I counted what I've saved in my piggy bank and my mother said I could bring you home."

"Shall I put him in a box for you?" the saleslady asked.

"Oh, no thank you," Lisa answered. And she carried Corduroy home in her arms.

She ran all the way up four flights of stairs, into her family's apartment, and straight to her own room.

Corduroy blinked. There was a chair
and a chest of drawers, and alongside a
girl-size bed stood a little bed just the
right size for him. The room was small,
nothing like that enormous palace in the
department store.

"This must be home," he said. "I *know*
I've always wanted a home!"

Lisa sat down with Corduroy on her lap
and began to sew a button on his overalls.
"I like you the way you are," she said,
"but you'll be more comfortable with your
shoulder strap fastened."

"You must be a friend," said Corduroy.
"I've always wanted a friend."

"Me too!" said Lisa, and gave him a
big hug.

Corduroy

Meet the Author and Illustrator

Don Freeman had a job playing the trumpet until he left his trumpet in the subway in New York City. He forgot his trumpet because he was so busy drawing for his art class. From then on, Freeman made his living drawing pictures. Freeman wrote and illustrated his first children's book for his young son, Roy. Many more books followed, including "Corduroy."

Theme Connections

Think About It

Did "Corduroy" teach you anything about kindness? Here are some ideas to help you:

- Would you choose Corduroy if you saw him in a store? Why or why not?
- Why did Lisa think that Corduroy was perfect for her?
- Was Lisa kind in a special way? How?
- Who else in the story was kind?
- Have you ever been kind in the same way as Lisa was?

Check the Concept/Question Board and answer any questions that you can. Post any questions you have.

Record Ideas

Pick one of the characters in the story. Think about all the feelings he or she had. Draw a picture of the character and print his or her name below. Print the feelings the character had all around your picture. Draw facial expressions of the feelings.

Draw a Thinking Picture

- Draw two Thought Balloons.
- Inside the balloons, draw two pictures—one that shows what Lisa was wishing and one that shows what Corduroy was wishing.

April Medicine

Joyce Carol Thomas
illustrated by Floyd Cooper

My mother's touch, so tender, so certain
Steadies me with healing hands
Hands that cool my brow when I perspire
And warm me when I shiver

My mother's hands already know
The temperature of my head
The weather of my heart
How do they know to be cool when I'm hot
And warm when I'm not?

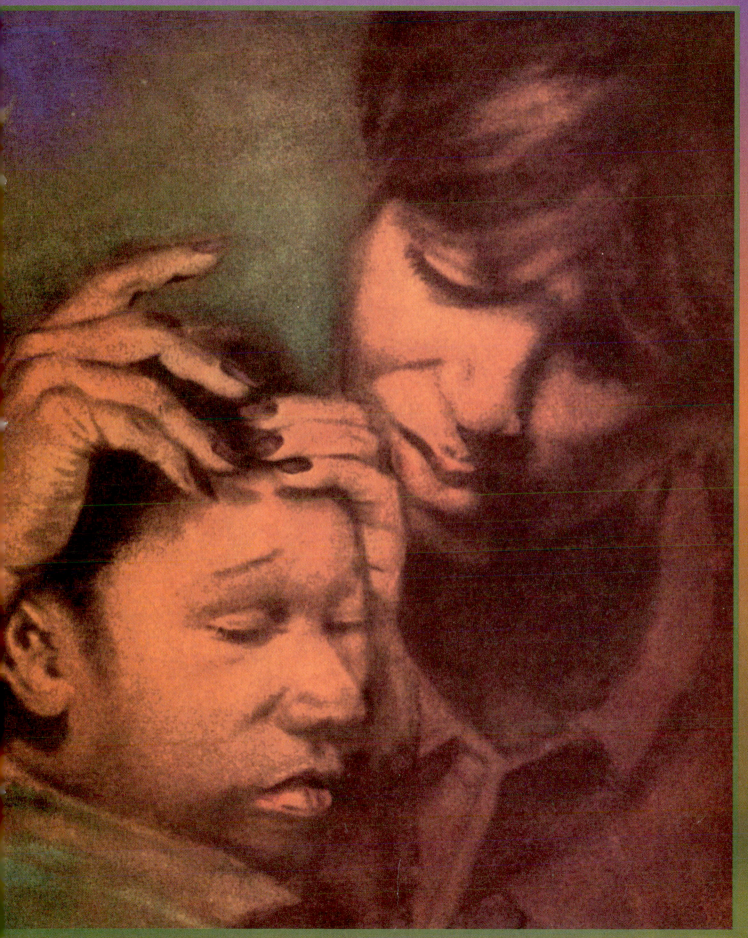

The Story of Three Whales

Giles Whittell

illustrated by Patrick Benson

For twelve bright weeks every summer, the Arctic Ocean is full of life. Blooms of plankton float among the icebergs. Shellfish slide along the sea floor. Squid lurk under pitch-black overhangs of rock. And whales swim up from the Pacific to feed.

Humpback whales, Bowhead whales and California Gray whales all come to the Arctic. In the summer of 1988 one particular herd of California Grays was plunging and rolling, leaping and belly-flopping, off the north coast of Alaska.

But winter came early in 1988. The first sign was a freezing wind from the east. Blizzards blew in from the top of the world. Thick pack-ice spread out from the shore and its shadow fell over the whales.

Most of the whales were quick to sense the changes. In small groups, they set off on the long swim south to warmth for the winter. But three of the whales failed to notice the end of summer—one adult, one middle-sized, one baby.

Quietly the ice crept in. The ocean was changing from blue to silent white. Gray whales hold their breath under water for half an hour, but soon the three who had been left behind would have no where left to surface.

Only the open water was safe, beyond the pack-ice. But the three whales lost their sense of direction. They swam toward land, into an Alaskan bay, where the still, shallow water was certain to freeze very quickly.

At the mouth of the bay was a shelf of ice, under water. Broken pack-ice piled up against it, forming a wall. From sea-bed to surface there was no way out.

Then the surface froze solid. The whales were trapped in a prison of ice. They could not breathe. Again and again they rammed upward at the ice with their noses.

At last they managed to push their great heads through a crack in the ice. An Inuit hunter was passing and saw them. In nearby Barrow, an Inuit town, he told people what he had seen.

To begin with nothing was done to save the whales. It would be natural for the whales to die and the Inuit accepted it. But the news of the whales began to spread. Their pictures appeared on local TV.

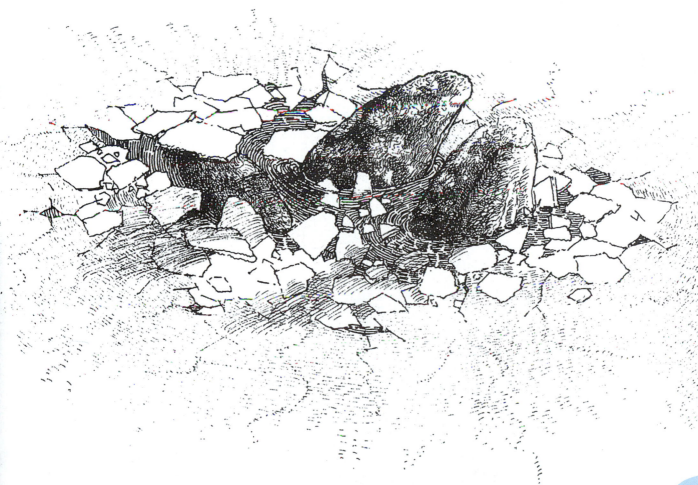

One person who heard the news was
a wildlife ranger. She persuaded the
people of Barrow to help keep the whales
alive. Out over the ice they trudged, with
axes, ice-poles and chainsaws to cut
breathing holes.

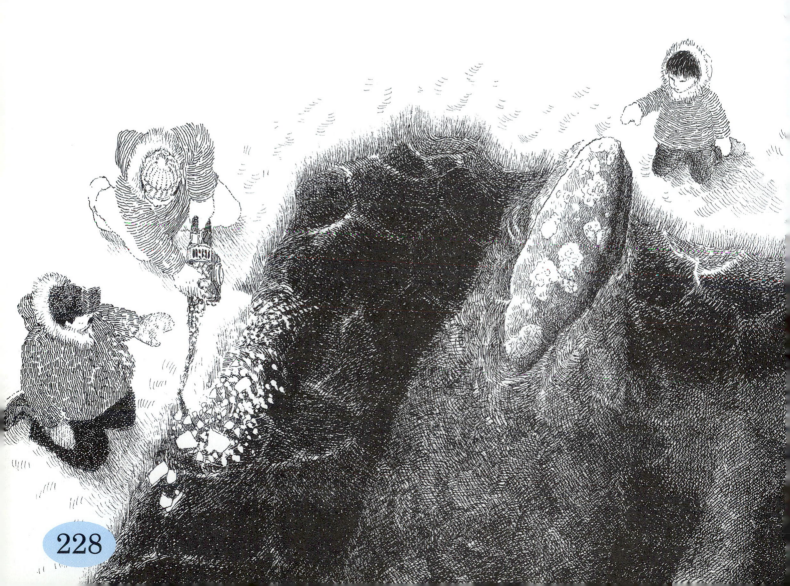

The whales appeared at the holes and filled their huge lungs. The Inuit gave them names: Siku (the biggest), Poutu (the middle one) and Kannick (the baby). *Siku* means ice in Inuit. *Poutu* means ice-hole and *Kannick* means snowflake.

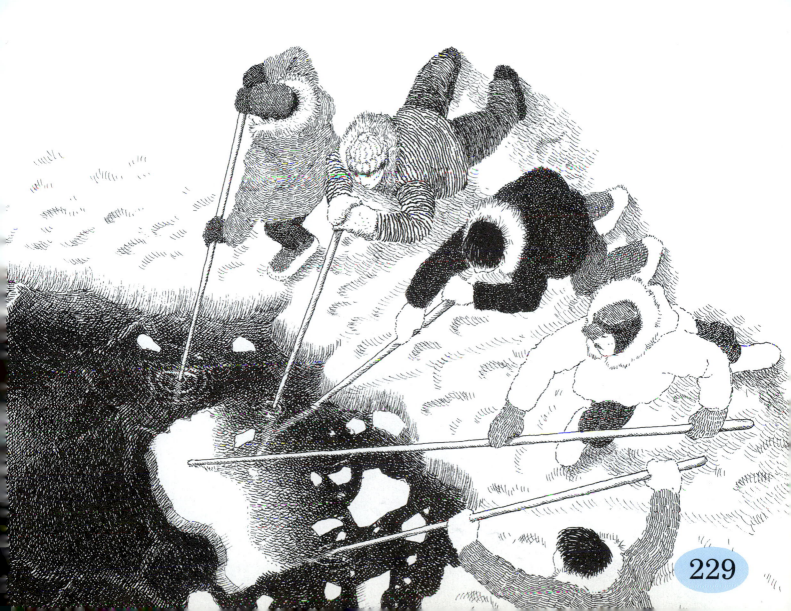

The Inuit cut a line of breathing holes, out toward the open water. They worked for fourteen days and nights. Clattering chainsaws sliced constantly through the ice, but the water would quickly freeze solid again.

Siku, Poutu and Kannick refused to follow the line of holes. They stayed by the shore where they knew they could breathe. "The Plight of the Whales" became front-page news all over the world. Millions of people waited in hope.

From all across America, offers of
help poured in. But nothing could break
through the wall of ice at the mouth of
the bay. An enormous bulldozer tried,
but stuck fast.

A sky-crane helicopter hammered the ice with a concrete torpedo. It punched a line of holes from the whales to the wall. But still the whales wouldn't follow.

Their noses were bloody and scraped to the bone. The ice was invincible. It seemed to the watching world that the whales must die. Polar bears stalked the ice, waiting patiently for a feast of whale-meat.

One evening Siku and Poutu surfaced alone. Being the smallest, Kannick was also the weakest. Morning came and still only Siku and Poutu appeared at the hole. No one could say exactly what had happened. And no one ever saw Kannick again.

On the twentieth day, Siku and Poutu felt the tremble of distant engines. A huge Russian ice-breaker was roaring to the rescue, the great *Admiral Makarov*.

The captain found a grand phrase to mark the occasion. "Let us begin to break ice!" he called. All night the breaker charged at the ice, pulled back, and charged again.

By morning a channel was clear, a quarter of a mile wide. The crew of the *Admiral Makarov* grinned. They came ashore to celebrate and the Inuit and other Americans hugged them and cheered.

Then the ice-breaker turned for the open sea with Siku and Poutu close behind. The whales understood that they must follow the thunder and froth of the engines. The sound would lead them from the prison of ice, to the open water and freedom.

The rest of the herd was three weeks ahead on the journey south. Siku and Poutu had thousands of miles to swim. So they each blew a great waterspout and set off.

Their long ordeal was over now.

The Story of Three Whales

Meet the Author

Giles Whittell grew up in Kenya, Nigeria, and Algeria. In 1989 he rode his bicycle from Berlin to Bulgaria and then wrote about his trip. He is a reporter for a newspaper in Los Angeles.

Meet the Illustrator

Patrick Benson was born and lives in England. He worked in filmmaking and sculpture before he began illustrating books for children. He has illustrated twenty-five children's books. *"What I really want is to get good pictures to as many children as possible."*

240

Theme Connections

Think About It

Many people working together were able to help the whales. Kindness can be shown by one or many. Here are some questions to think about:

- Why did the people care about the whales?
- Were you afraid the whales would not get free? Why?
- Do you know any other true stories where people were kind to animals? How were they the same as or different from this story?
- What would you do if you saw an animal that needed help?

Check the Concept/Question Board and answer any questions that you can. Post any new questions you have.

Record Ideas

 With a partner, make a list of all the ideas in the story to help the whales. Draw a light bulb with an "**X**" beside each idea that did not work. Do you remember what this icon tells us?

Draw a Picture

Work with your partner and think of an idea that you would try to help the whales. Draw a picture of your idea.

The Whales' Song

Dyan Sheldon

illustrated by Gary Blythe

Lilly's grandmother told her a story.

"Once upon a time," she said, "the ocean
was filled with whales. They were as big as
the hills. They were as peaceful as the moon.
They were the most wondrous creatures you
could ever imagine."

Lilly climbed onto her grandmother's lap.

"I used to sit at the end of the pier and listen for whales," said Lilly's grandmother. "Sometimes I'd sit there all day and all night. Then suddenly I'd see them coming toward me from miles away. They moved through the water as if they were dancing."

"But why did they swim to you, Grandma?" asked Lilly. "How did they know you were there?"

Lilly's grandmother smiled. "Oh, you had to bring them something special. A perfect shell. Or a beautiful stone. And if they liked you, the whales would take your gift and give you something in return."

"What would they give you, Grandma?" asked Lilly. "What did you get from the whales?"

Lilly's grandmother sighed. "Once or twice," she whispered, "once or twice, I heard them sing."

Lilly's great-uncle Frederick stomped into the room. "That's nothing but a silly old tale!" he snapped. "Whales were important for their meat, and for their bones, and for their blubber. If you have to tell Lilly about whales, then tell her something useful. Don't fill her head with nonsense. Singing whales, indeed!"

247

"There were whales here millions of years before there were ships, or cities, or even cave dwellers," continued Lilly's grandmother. "People used to say they were magical."

"People used to eat them and boil them down for oil!" grumbled Lilly's great-uncle Frederick. And he stomped back out of the room.

Lilly dreamt about whales.

In her dreams she saw them, as large as mountains and bluer than the sky. In her dreams she heard them singing, their voices like the wind. In her dreams they leapt from the water and called her name.

In the morning Lilly went down to the ocean, to the place where no one fished or swam or sailed. She walked to the end of the old pier. The water was empty and still. She took a yellow flower out of her pocket and dropped it in the water.

"This is for you," she called into the air.

Lilly sat at the end of the pier and waited.

She waited all morning and all afternoon.

Then, as dusk began to fall, Uncle Frederick came down the hill after her. "Enough of this foolishness," he said. "Come on home. You can't be dreaming your life away."

That night Lilly awoke suddenly.

The room was bright with moonlight.
She sat up and listened. The house was quiet.
Lilly climbed out of bed and went to the
window. She could hear something in the
distance, on the far side of the hill.

She raced outside and down to the shore. Her heart was pounding as she reached the sea.

There, enormous in the ocean, were the whales.

They leapt and jumped and spun across the moon.

Their singing filled the night.

Lilly saw her yellow flower dancing on the spray.

Minutes passed, or maybe hours. Suddenly Lilly felt the breeze rustle her nightgown and the cold nip at her toes. She shivered and rubbed her eyes. Then it seemed the ocean was still again and the night dark and silent.

Lilly thought she must have been dreaming. She stood up and turned toward home. Then from far, far away, on the breath of the wind, she heard "Lilly! Lilly!"

The whales were calling her name.

The Whales' Song

Meet the Author

Dyan Sheldon and her family moved from the city to the shores of Long Island when she was seven. This move was not easy. It was not until her mother found an arrowhead in their backyard that she began to enjoy her home in a new way. *"The arrowhead was the first thing to make both the past and present real."*

Dyan Sheldon would often watch schools of porpoise swim off the shore. She wrote *The Whales' Song* when she learned that many dolphins and whales are in danger from the nets of fishermen.

Meet the Illustrator

Gary Blythe was born in England. He came to the United States with his wife to study the Native Americans in South Dakota. He has created sketches, photographs, and oil paintings of the Dakota countryside. He now lives in England and works as an artist. *"I enjoy doing dreamlike images,"* said Gary Blythe. He likes to make fantasy look real. *The Whales' Song* is his first picture book.

Theme Connections

Think About It

Do you think that the man in the story was mean? Here are some questions to help you decide:

- Why did he think the grandmother shouldn't tell Lilly the stories about the whales?
- Why didn't he want Lilly to watch and wait for the whales?
- Was the man telling Lilly and her grandmother to stop talking about the whales just to be mean or did he have another reason? What might his reason be?

Record Ideas

Do you think the illustrations make this story better? Why or why not? Record your ideas in your Writing Journal.

Draw a Picture

This story has many "word pictures"—groups of words that help us imagine how something looks. For example, Lilly's grandmother said that the whales moved "through the water as if they were dancing." Pick your favorite "word picture" and illustrate it.

Cinderella

retold by Fabio Coen

illustrated by Lane Yerkes

Once there was a girl who was very kind
and patient. Her wicked stepmother called
her Cinderella because she often sat by the
fireplace close to the cinders.

Her stepmother made her work all day long. She had to light the fire, prepare the meals, wash the dishes, clean the house, and make beautiful gowns for her two stepsisters, who were very ugly and very mean.

Cinderella was always dressed in rags, but she
was more beautiful in her rags than her
stepsisters in their beautiful gowns.

One day the King and Queen gave a ball.
Cinderella helped her stepmother and her
stepsisters to get ready. Then the three of them
went to the ball.

Cinderella was all alone. She began to cry.
Suddenly her Fairy Godmother appeared. "Why
are you crying?" she asked Cinderella.

"I, too, would have liked to go to the ball,"
Cinderella replied.

"Then you shall go," said her Fairy Godmother. "Bring me a pumpkin from the garden."

With one touch of her magic wand, Cinderella's Fairy Godmother turned the pumpkin into a beautiful carriage. Then she took six mice from a trap. A touch of the magic wand turned them into six prancing horses. In the cellar Cinderella's Fairy Godmother found a large rat. She turned him into a large coachman with a great mustache.

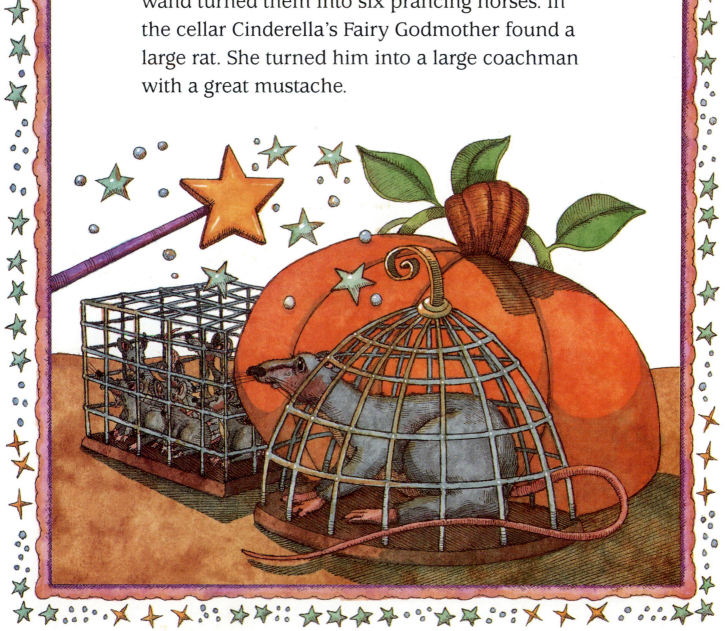

265

Another touch of the magic wand and Cinderella's rags turned into a beautiful silver gown covered with diamonds. On her feet were a pair of little glass slippers.

As she stepped into the carriage, her Fairy Godmother said, "Have a good time, but remember this. You must leave the ball before midnight. When the clock strikes twelve, your carriage will turn into a pumpkin, your horses into mice, your coachman into a rat, and your gown into rags."

Cinderella promised to leave the ball before midnight. Then they drove away.

Cinderella was so beautiful that the prince danced with her all night. She forgot about her Fairy Godmother's warning. The clock began to strike twelve. Cinderella ran out of the palace and down the stairs. In her hurry she lost one of her glass slippers.

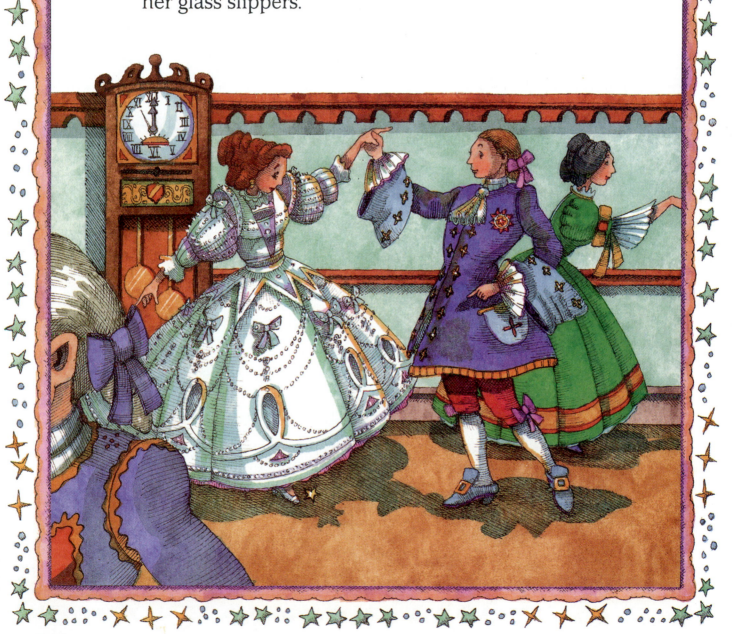

The prince ran after Cinderella, but it was too late. By the time he reached the bottom of the stairs, her beautiful carriage was gone. The prince found only her little glass slipper.

The prince had fallen in love with Cinderella. He wanted to find her, but he didn't even know her name or where she lived. He sent a page to every house in the kingdom. In each house the page asked every girl to try on the slipper. But their feet were much too big for the tiny slipper.

At last the page came to the house where
Cinderella lived. Her two stepsisters hurried to
try on the little slipper. But their feet were much
too big. No matter how hard they tried, they
could not get the slipper on.

Then it was Cinderella's turn. The slipper fit her perfectly. At that moment her Fairy Godmother appeared and dressed Cinderella in a gown of shimmering gold.

Cinderella and the prince were married. Because she was so kind, Cinderella forgave her wicked stepmother and stepsisters, and they all lived happily ever after.

Cinderella

Meet the Author

Fabio Coen was born in Rome, Italy. He came to the United States in 1940 and later became a citizen. He loved books and went to work for a publishing company. While he worked there he helped other authors of children's books get started.

Meet the Illustrator

Lane Yerkes has created illustrations for advertising, newspapers, magazines, textbooks, and logos. He has written and illustrated two children's stories that he hopes to publish. His home is located on the southwest coast of Florida, just above the Everglades. He lives with his wife and their dog. When not working, he enjoys boating and fishing.

Theme Connections

Think About It

Here are some questions about kindness:

- Why do you think Cinderella's stepmother and stepsisters were so mean to her?
- If you were Cinderella, would you have forgiven the stepmother and stepsisters? Why or why not?
- Is it hard to be kind to people who are not kind to you? Why?

Check the Concept/Question Board and answer any questions that you can.

Record Ideas

How would a modern-day story be different? Write your ideas in your Writing Journal.

Perform a Story

Make a "modern-day" version of the story. What details could you change?

- Where do you think Cinderella might go, instead of to the ball?
- What might she ride in instead of a coach?
- Who might she meet, instead of a prince?
- Perform your modern-day Cinderella story. Decide who will be the narrators and the characters. Decide what the characters will say. Practice before you perform your story.

Bibliography

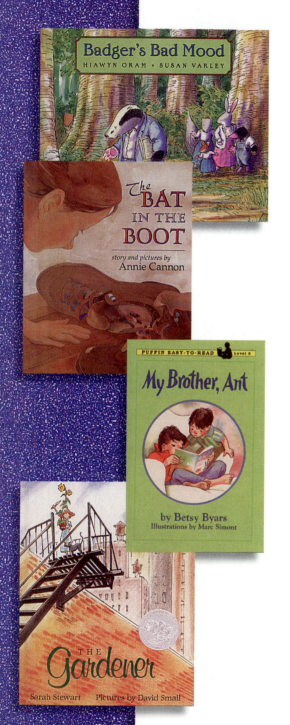

Badger's Bad Mood

by Hiawyn Oram. What plan does Mole come up with to chase his best friend Badger's blues away?

The Bat in the Boot

by Annie Cannon. The bats come at night, so why is there a bat in a boot in broad daylight?

My Brother, Ant

by Betsy Byars. Anthony's big brother is kind to him in many ways.

The Gardener

by Sarah Stewart. What changes does Lydia make to the rooftop of her Uncle Jim's bakery hoping to make him smile? Read and see how kindness blooms!

I Know a Lady

by Charlotte Zolotow. Sally knows a lady who is always doing something nice for someone else. Would you like to meet her?

Jamaica's Find

by Juanita Havill. Is it really better to give than to receive? In Jamaica's case, it is better to give back.

Leah's Pony

by Elizabeth Friedrich. What is Leah willing to part with to help her family through hard times? What would you be willing to give up?

Tonio's Cat

by Mary Calhoun. Why does Tonio's kindness to a stray cat, Toughy, make him happier in his new country?

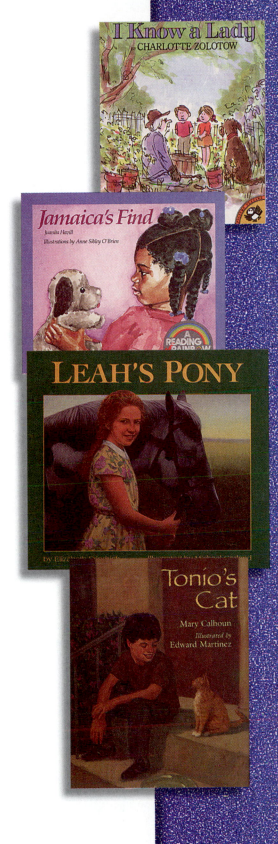

Seeing is believing. Or is it? Can you always trust what you see? Can something look like one thing and really be something different? Maybe!

I See Animals Hiding

by Jim Arnosky

I see animals hiding. I see a porcupine high in a tree.

Wild animals are shy and always hiding. It is natural for them to be this way. There are many dangers in the wild.

Even when they are caught unaware out in the open, wild animals try to hide. They stay behind whatever is available—a thin tree trunk or even a single blade of grass. Most of the time they go unnoticed.

The colors of wild animals match the colors of the places where the animals live. Because of this protective coloration, called camouflage, wild animals can hide by simply staying still and blending in.

Woodcocks and other birds, which spend much of their time on the woodland floor, have patterns and colors like those of dry leaves.

I see animals hiding. I see two woodcocks on the leafy ground.

Of all wild animals, deer are the wariest. Even though their colors are camouflaged, they feel safe only where there are good hiding places nearby.

In a summer meadow of tall grasses and small shrubby trees, deer can hide quickly by just lying down.

**There are 20 deer on the snowy hill.
Can you find them all?**

In autumn, deer shed their red-brown summer coats and replace them with warmer, grayer winter coats that better match the gray and brown trunks of leafless trees.

I see animals hiding. I see a whole herd of deer on a winter hill.

Snowshoe hares change from summer brown to winter white. The only way to spot a snowshoe hare in a snowy scene is to look for its shiny black eyes.

Squint your eyes and you will see just how invisible a snowshoe hare on snow can be.

Here are three more animals that are as white as snow. The arctic fox and long-tailed weasel change from winter white to summer brown. The snowy owl stays white year-round.

The colors and patterns of screech owls blend perfectly with tree bark. These small owls can sleep all day out in the open and not be discovered.

Besides an owl, there is one other bark imitator on this tree. Can you tell what it is?

I see animals hiding. I see an owl and a moth on a limb.

Trout are camouflaged by color and shape to blend with the smooth mossy stones in a stream.

Looking down in a brook, I see a speckled trout swimming amid speckled stones.

I see animals hiding. I see a garter snake slithering through the grass.

Up close a snake in the grass may be easy to see. But as long as the snake keeps a safe distance from its enemies, it can sneak by, looking like just another broken branch on the ground.

Stand back a few steps from this page, and using only your eyes, try to follow the line of the snake from its head to its tail. Can you tell what is snake and what is stick?

A bittern is a wading bird whose brown streaks and long sticklike legs naturally blend in with the cattails and reeds that grow along shorelines.

When a bittern really needs to be invisible, it points its bill upward and sways its long neck, like a cattail swaying gently in a breeze.

And last but not least:
Animals hide by staying inside.

I See Animals Hiding

Meet the Author and Illustrator

James Edward Arnosky and his family live in the northern Vermont wilderness. He observes nature while fishing, drawing, or walking. His illustrations try to teach readers how to see as an artist would.

"I write about the world I live in and try to share all I see and feel in my books." Arnosky often describes the natural world in a way that the reader becomes a part of the scene. He sums up the role of an author saying, *"The best nonfiction lets the reader knock on the door, and you let them in. Then you go away."*

Theme Connections

Think About It

What does the information in "I See Animals Hiding" have to do with Look Again? Here are some questions to think about and discuss:

- Why is it sometimes difficult to spot animals in a natural setting?
- Why do animals need to hide?
- What other things can you think of that you have to look closely at to really see them?

Post any questions you have about the theme Look Again on the Concept/Question Board.

Record Ideas

Record in your Writing Journal any thoughts about the questions above that you talked about with others. You may choose to simply list your ideas or to present them in a chart form.

Make a Mural

- Work with a partner or a small group.
- Draw or paste pictures of animals onto a large sheet of paper.
- Draw and color the surroundings so that the animals are camouflaged.
- Share your mural with another group and find the hidden animals on the other group's mural.

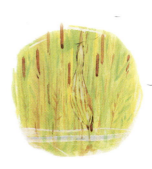

Animal Camouflage

by Janet McDonnell

What Is Camouflage?

Have you ever played hide and seek outside? Sometimes it is hard to find a good place to hide! But what if you could paint yourself brown and green like the ground?

Or put on a costume that made you look like a tree? Or lie down and cover yourself with leaves? All of these tricks would make you much harder to find.

A forest looks green and brown.

What Is Camouflage?

Some animals use tricks to hide themselves. Using colors and patterns to hide is called **camouflage.** Camouflage makes things very hard to find—even when they are out in the open.

A walkingstick looks like the branches around it.

Animals, fish, reptiles, and even people use camouflage for hiding. When something looks like the objects around it, it is much harder to see. That is what camouflage is all about!

Why Do Animals Need Camouflage?

There are many reasons why animals hide. They often hide from their enemies. Some animals move around at night and sleep during the day. They need to stay hidden while they sleep.

This emperor moth has an eyespot on its wing to scare enemies.

Other animals hide so that they can be
better hunters. Camouflage helps them
sneak up on their dinner.

How Do Animals Use Camouflage?

Animals use camouflage in many different ways. Some use it to blend in with the objects around them. These objects are called **surroundings.** The *polar bear's* white coat blends in with its surroundings—the white snow. This color hides the bear when it is hunting for seals.

The white fur of this polar bear looks like the snow around it.

The *black bear's* dark coat helps it hide in dark trees and bushes.

But what happens if an animal's surroundings are more than one color? Some animals have camouflage with more than one color, too!

Some fish have dark backs and white bellies. When a hungry bird looks into the dark water, the fish's dark back is hard to see. But to an enemy deeper in the water, the fish's white belly blends in with the bright sky.

This large mouth bass has a dark back that matches the water.

Why Do Some Animals Change Color?

Sometimes an animal's surroundings change. Then the animal has to change color, too! That is the only way it can stay hidden. Some animals change color to match the season. The *snowshoe rabbit* changes color very slowly in the spring and fall.

In the winter, the snowshoe rabbit's fur is white like the snow. As the snow melts in the spring, the rabbit grows patches of brown fur. It looks just like patches of ground and melting snow.

This snowshoe rabbit has white fur to match the snow.

Then summer comes, and the ground is brown. The rabbit's fur grows brown to match. When fall comes, the rabbit starts to turn white again.

This baby snowshoe rabbit has brown fur in the spring.

Do All Animals Use Colors to Hide?

Some animals use designs, or **patterns,** instead of changing colors. Blending into a pattern is a good way to hide. When an animal's body looks like its surroundings, it is very hard to find.

A *fawn*, or baby deer, is too weak to run fast. But it can hide by lying still. The fawn's back is covered with dots. The dots look like spots of sunlight on the forest floor. If the fawn stays still, it is very hard to see.

Fawns like this one can blend into their surroundings.

Another animal that uses patterns to hide is the *bittern*. This bird lives in marshes with tall grass. The stripes on its feathers look just like shadows in the grass.

This bittern has patterns that match the tall grass.

When the bittern is in danger, it makes itself even harder to find. It points its beak straight up and sways its body in the breeze. The bittern looks just like the blowing grass!

What Is Mimicry?

Some animals have a shape or color that looks like something else. This type of camouflage is called **mimicry.** Animals that use mimicry are good pretenders.

The *walkingstick* is one insect that uses mimicry. Its long, thin, bumpy body looks just like a small branch!

This walkingstick looks like a branch.

Walkingsticks can even change color with the seasons. In the spring, the tree's branches and leaves are green. The walkingstick is green, too. When the branches and leaves turn brown, the walkingstick turns brown to match.

Some animals use other kinds of mimicry to fool their enemies. Some moths have large spots on their rear wings. The spots look just like eyes!

When the moth is resting, its front wings cover the spots. But when the moth senses danger, it lifts its front wings and shows the spots. If an enemy is afraid of the big "eyes," it will leave the moth alone.

The spots on this Io moth's wings look like eyes.

Some animals even make their own costumes for camouflage. The *masked crab* uses seaweed to make a costume.

This masked crab has used many things to make its costume.

First the crab uses its claws to tear the seaweed into pieces. Then it puts each piece in its mouth and chews it until it is soft. The crab sticks the pieces of seaweed to itself. Little hooks on its shell and legs hold the seaweed in place.

From a rabbit that changes color to a crab in a seaweed costume, there are many kinds of camouflage. But each kind of camouflage has the same important job—to help animals hide.

This zale moth is hard to see because it looks like the tree trunk.

Now that you know some of their tricks, maybe you will see animals where you never saw them before. But you'll have to look very carefully, or you might be fooled!

Animal Camouflage

Meet the Author

Janet McDonnell came up with the idea for writing "Animal Camouflage" during a brainstorming session with publishers. Since she loves animals, she was excited to be given the chance to write about them. When she writes about a subject, she likes to research it very carefully. Sometimes she gets so much information that she cannot use it because the book can only be so long. Then her challenge is to get the ideas across in a clear and interesting way. *"My goal is to make the reader as excited about the topic as I am,"* she said.

Theme Connections

Think About It

What new things have you learned about animal camouflage? Discuss the following questions with a group of classmates:

- What are some of the different ways that animals use camouflage?
- Why are some animals so colorful or have special markings?
- Which animals were the most difficult to find in the photographs?

Check the Concept/Question Board and answer any questions you can. Post new questions you have about the theme Look Again.

Record Ideas

 Record in your Writing Journal any new information you learned about animal camouflage. You may choose to simply list your ideas or to present them in a chart form.

Make a Chart

- Make a chart of the different headings in the story.
- Below each heading, give short answers to the question asked in the heading.
- For example, the first heading is "What Is Camouflage?" Write a short answer to that question using examples given in the story.

What Color Is Camouflage?

Carolyn Otto

illustrated by Megan Lloyd

In the foothills near my house, a mountain lion might be hunting. He stalks across a dry hillside. His golden fur matches the grass.

A doe raises her head to sniff the air. Her fawn is quiet, and the lion passes by.

Mountain Lion

Mule Deer

American Robin

Striped Skunks

In my backyard, a robin could catch an insect that looks like a leaf.

After dark, a skunk and her babies might walk right down my street. My dog can see their bold white stripes, but he's learned to leave skunks alone.

Bobcat

Great Horned Owl

Field Mice

Yellow-Bellied Marmots

Short Horned Lizard

Near my house, and all over the world, at every time of day or night, animals are hunting for food . . . or they are being hunted.

Animals must eat in order to live, and to live they sometimes have to hide. Animals hide in holes, burrows, and dens, in plants, underwater, and beneath rocks.

Mountain Lion

Mule Deer

Some animals hide out in plain sight,
but they are still very hard to see. The
doe's coat and the mountain lion's fur
blend into the colors surrounding them.

Mule Deer Fawn

---◆---

The fawn's spots match the sun and shade that dapple the thicket where she hides. When in danger, the fawn must stay very still. Any movement might draw the eye of the hunter.

The fawn and the doe, and the prowling lion—each one of these animals is camouflaged.

---◆---

Red Fox

Eastern Chipmunks

What color is camouflage? Camouflage can be a certain color, or pattern of colors, or a special shape that fools the eye. Animal camouflage is a kind of disguise. It makes an animal hard to see.

Camouflage helps an animal hide from enemies, and it can help a hunter sneak up on its prey.

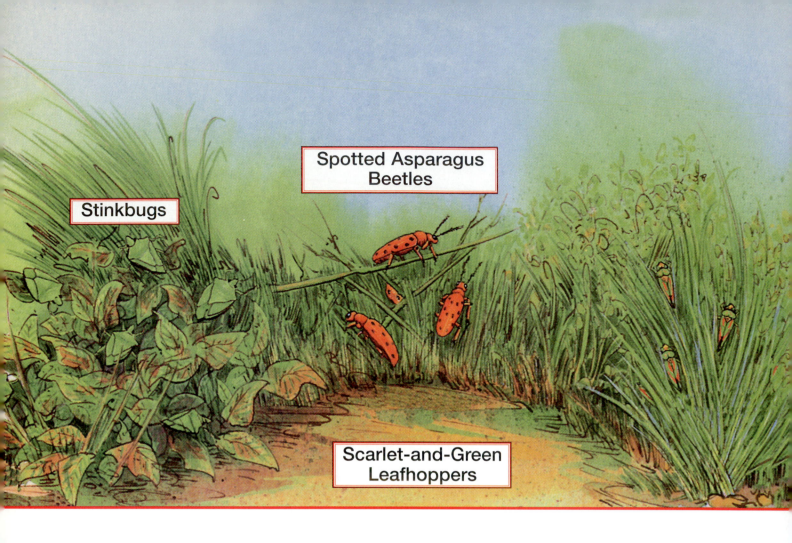

Stinkbugs

Spotted Asparagus
Beetles

Scarlet-and-Green
Leafhoppers

Hiding and hunting are both made easier when an animal matches its surroundings. A green insect clinging to a green leaf is much harder to see than a red insect. If a green insect is shaped like a leaf, even the hungriest bird could miss it.

Hermit Crab

Some animals disguise themselves by dressing in plants, pebbles, even other living things. Many crabs are experts at decorating their bodies with seaweed, shells, rocks, sponges, or anemones.

Lesser Sponge Crab

Stick Insect

Red Bat

Common Poorwill

When animals are perfectly camouflaged, sticks seem to crawl, leaves can fly, and a stone may have eyes and a beak.

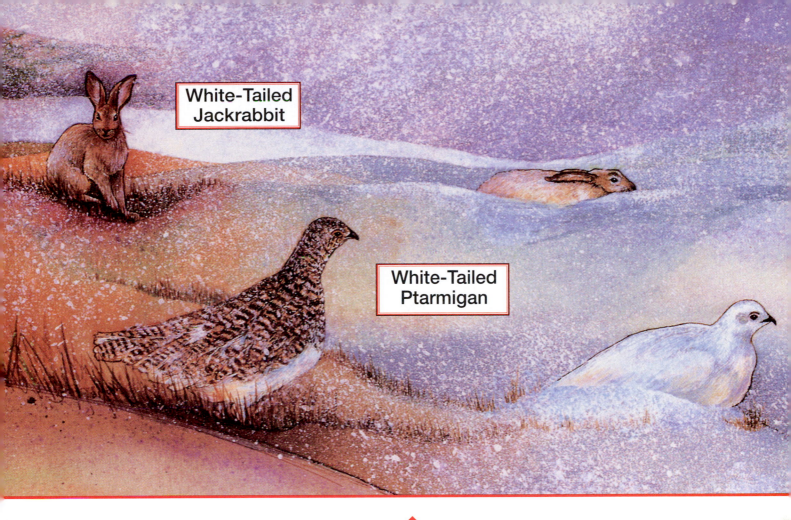

White-Tailed Jackrabbit

White-Tailed Ptarmigan

High up in the mountains above my house, this rock-colored ptarmigan warms her eggs. In summer, a ptarmigan has many dark feathers. By snowfall, her feathers will be pure white.

When the surrounding world changes color, certain animals can change right along. Some, like the ptarmigan, change slowly. Her feathers change color as she molts.

Only the dark eyes and tips of his ears give away a jackrabbit in his winter coat.

Mule Deer

Young animals may change coloring as they grow—as they get big, or strong, or very swift.

The fawn's spots will gradually fade, when she can run away from danger.

Green Anoles

Common Atlantic Octopus

Though it may take nearly three minutes for an American anole to change coloring, certain chameleons, squids, and octopuses can turn different colors in seconds flat. They may change to match their surroundings, or because they feel excited or threatened.

American Robins

◆

Many animals don't ever change.
Some don't need any camouflage.
These animals don't have to hide.
Their colors may attract attention.

A robin's red breast helps him find a
mate, and a skunk's bold stripes are a
warning.

◆

Spotted Skunk

Yellow Jacket

Gila Monster

Animals sometimes use colors or bright patterns to say:

"I smell,"

"I sting,"

or "I'm poisonous."

Bobcat

Spotted Skunk

Once sprayed by a skunk or stung by a bee, a hunter learns to avoid them next time.

332

Harmful	**Harmless**

Honey Bee	Hover Fly

Arizona Coral Snake	Organ Pipe Shovel-Nosed Snake
	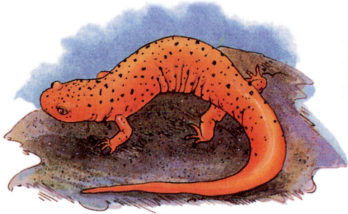
Eastern Newt	Red Salamander

Harmless animals may copy warning signals to protect themselves from their enemies.

Black Swallowtail

Buckeye

Common Toad

A flash of bright color may be enough to fool a predator, or to scare it away. Some animals have spots that look like eyes. Eyespots can frighten or confuse an enemy. A hunter may strike at "eyes" on a wing or tail, which gives the prey a small chance to escape.

Gray Treefrog

Green Lacewing

Praying Mantis

Whether hunter or hunted, predator or prey, colors and camouflage help an animal survive.

Queen Hornet Wasp

Black Widow Spider

Wherever you live, animals live near you.

In backyards and in city parks, outside and inside your house, in plants, underwater, in air, animals are everywhere.

Pine Grosbeak

Spotted Skunk

Do you see an animal?

An animal you can spot right away may be saying something important.

Smooth Green Snake

Oak Inchworm
Caterpillar

Flammulated Owl

Snapping Turtle

Western Toad

Buffalo Treehopper

Look closely, and more closely still.
Look at colors, patterns, and shapes:

an old stump could be a bird,
a green branch may be a snake,
a twig might be a caterpillar,
a thorn might be an insect,
a rock may be a turtle,
a dead leaf could be a toad.

Look closely when you go outside.
Can you find the hidden animals?

When animals are camouflaged,
they can be very hard to see.

What Color Is Camouflage?

Meet the Author

Carolyn Otto worked for many years for a publishing firm in New York. She now writes children's books and lives in Colorado Springs, Colorado.

Meet the Illustrator

Megan Lloyd grew up in Pennsylvania and dreamed of becoming a ballerina. When she found out that her short height would keep her from becoming a ballerina, she began to think of a career in art. Her mother suggested she illustrate picture books. Lloyd began illustrating books soon after graduation from art school. *"The more I learn about illustrating books, the more I discover all that I don't know! . . . Each book presents a new puzzle to solve."*

Theme Connections

Think About It

What new information did you learn about animal camouflage from this selection? Here are some questions to think about:

- What color is camouflage?
- Where are some places you go that animals hide?
- What are all the uses of camouflage?
- What things do you look at again to get a better picture? Why?

Check the Concept/Question Board and answer any questions you can. Post any new questions you have about the theme Look Again.

Record Ideas

Record in your Writing Journal the color of camouflage for different animals. You may write down your ideas in a list, chart, or short paragraph.

Make a Diary

- Choose an animal that uses camouflage.
- Write a short diary about what a day might be like for that animal.
- Make sure you say when and why the animal would need camouflage.
- Illustrate your story with pictures.

FINE Art

Exotic Landscape. 1910. **Henri Rousseau.** Oil on canvas.
Norton Simon Foundation, Pasadena, California.

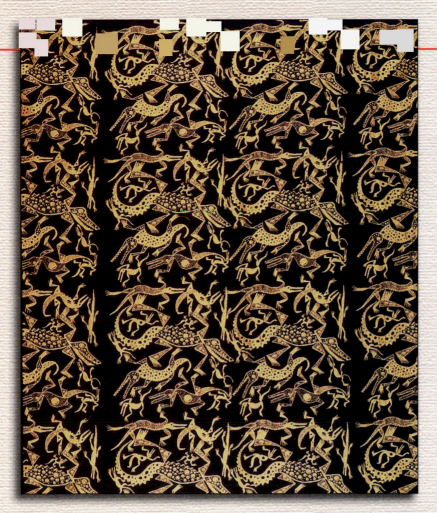

Printed Fabric from Bambalulu Handcraft Center. 1993. **Artist unknown.** Cotton with gold fabric ink. $2 \times 2\frac{1}{2}$ feet. Private Collection. Photo: © Tom Amedis.

Deidre. 1982. **Wendy Fay Dixon.** Silverpoint on paper. $17\frac{3}{4} \times 17$ in. The National Museum of Women in the Arts, Washington, D.C. Gift of Deidre Busenberg and the artist.

They Thought They Saw Him

Craig Kee Strete

illustrated by José Aruego and Ariane Dewey

L ittle dark chameleon crept out of the heart of his winter home and moved up onto a tiny branch.

Rain puddles glistened beneath his feet. The wind blew warm over the walls of the adobe. All winter little dark chameleon had lived, safe and asleep, beneath the granary where the people kept their seed corn.

Now insects buzzed over bush and tree, and he was awake.

As he moved on quick, silent feet, he began to forget the sleepy winter dark and felt now the joy in the first wakeful light of spring.

Eyes half closed, still filled with winter memories, little dark chameleon sat on a brown branch and waited for an insect to find his tongue.

A hungry snake watched him. The snake climbed the tree to catch the dark chameleon for his first meal of the spring.

But when he got there, everything on the brown branch was brown.

"The dark chameleon got away," said the snake, and he slithered off.

Little brown chameleon jumped off the
brown branch. His feet gripped green leaves,
and he hung there. His sticky tongue caught
a bug.

An owl, flying home to sleep, saw the brown chameleon in the green leaves. The owl swooped down to catch him.

But when he got there, everything in the green leaves was green.

"The brown chameleon got away," hooted the owl, and he flew off.

Little green chameleon jumped out of the green leaves and landed softly in the tan, rain-washed sand.

A fox saw the green chameleon in the sand. With pointed ears and hungry eyes, the fox crept toward him.

But when he got there, everything in the tan sand was tan.

"The green chameleon got away," yipped the fox, and he ran off.

Little tan chameleon crawled up on a ridge of golden rock.

An Apache boy saw the tan chameleon and tried to sneak up and catch him for a spring surprise.

But when he got there, everything on the golden rock was golden.

"The tan chameleon got away," said the boy, and he slowly walked off.

Little winter-dark, brown, green, tan, and golden chameleon warmed himself in the sunlight.

Snake, owl, fox, and boy all thought they saw him.

But little chameleon had his secret.

"Nobody sees me," he said, "because I am the color of the world."

They Thought They Saw Him

Meet the Author

Craig Kee Strete writes fiction for children and adults. He also writes for theater, television, and film. Strete's writing often describes the lives of young Native Americans growing up between two cultures. He shows the culture of the Native Americans and their love of nature. "They Thought They Saw Him" is a story that introduces Strete's world to others.

Meet the Illustrators

José Aruego and Ariane Dewey have combined their talents and have illustrated more than sixty children's books. Mr. Aruego does the drawings and Ms. Dewey adds the color through paint.

José Aruego began a career in law, but after a few months he realized that he wanted to draw, not practice law. After graduating from art school, he began drawing cartoons and later began illustrating children's books.

Ariane Dewey always loved bright colors. In fourth grade art class, she painted bright pink kids swimming in a blue-green lake. Her love of joyful colors is seen in many children's books.

Theme Connections

Think About It

Chameleons have a special kind of camouflage. Here are some questions to discuss:

- What sort of camouflage does the chameleon use?
- How does a chameleon's camouflage differ from other animals?
- What does the chameleon mean when he says he is "the color of the world"?

Check the Concept/Question Board and answer any questions you can. Post any new questions you have.

Record Ideas

 Record in your Writing Journal any ideas you have about chameleons and their camouflage. Tell how this story is different from the other selections in the unit.

Make a List

- Make a list of the places chameleon went and the colors he became.
- Then, underneath that, list places you doubt chameleon could go because camouflaging might be too difficult.
- Give each list a title.

The Chameleon

John Gardner
illustrated by Susan Nethery

People say the Chameleon can take on
the hue
Of whatever he happens to be on.
It's true
—Within reason, of course. If you put him
on plaid
Or polka dots, he really gets mad.

Caterpillar

Christina Rossetti
illustrated by Susan Nethery

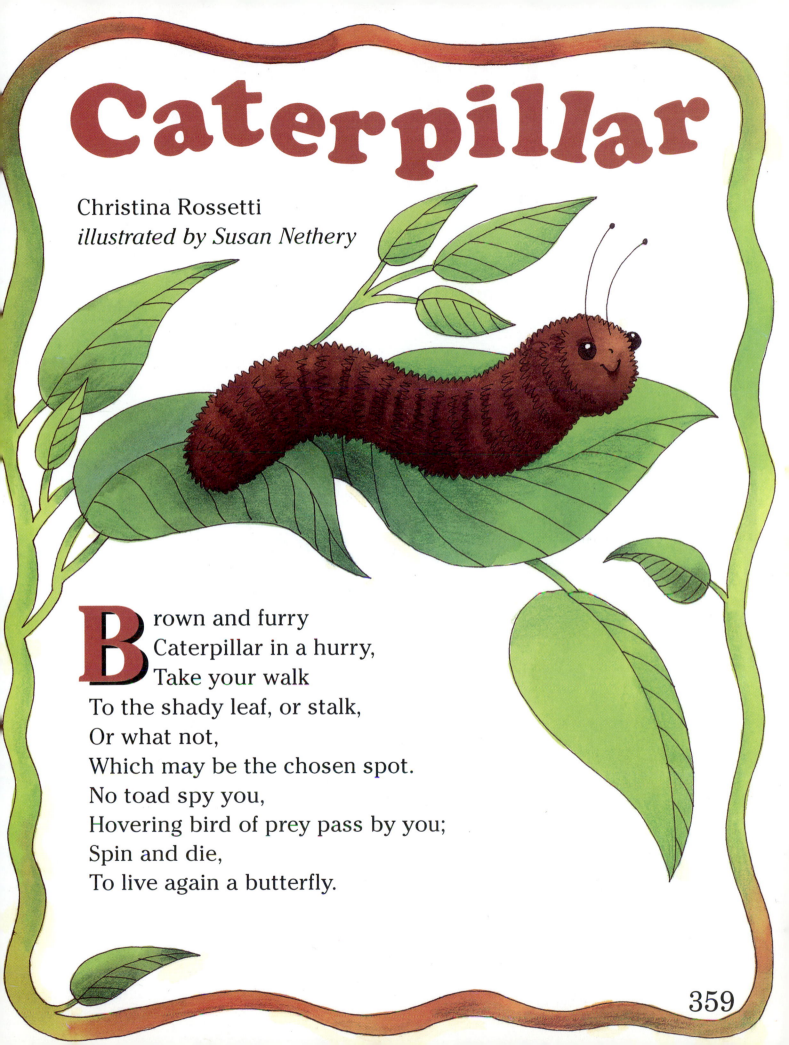

Brown and furry
Caterpillar in a hurry,
Take your walk
To the shady leaf, or stalk,
Or what not,
Which may be the chosen spot.
No toad spy you,
Hovering bird of prey pass by you;
Spin and die,
To live again a butterfly.

How the Guinea Fowl Got Her Spots

retold and illustrated by Barbara Knutson

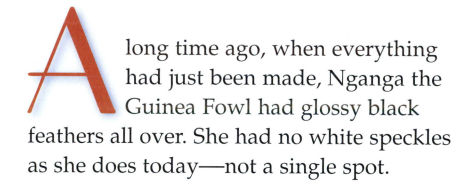

A long time ago, when everything had just been made, Nganga the Guinea Fowl had glossy black feathers all over. She had no white speckles as she does today—not a single spot.

Guinea Fowl was a little bird, but she had a big friend. And that was Cow.

They liked to go to the great green hills where Cow could eat grass and Nganga could scratch for seeds and crunch grasshoppers.

And they would both keep an eye out for Lion.

One day, Guinea Fowl was crossing the river to meet Cow on the most delicious hill they knew. The grass was so juicy and thick that, even from the river, Nganga could hear Cow hungrily tearing up one mouthful after another.

But . . . what was that Nganga saw slinking toward Cow?

Was it . . . ?

Yes, it was LION!

Now you might think a guinea fowl is no match for a lion, but Nganga didn't think that. In fact, she didn't think at all.

363

She scratched and scrambled up the bank as fast as she could and whirred right between Cow and Lion, kicking and flapping in the dust.

"RAAUGH!" shouted Lion.

"My eyes! This sand! What was that?"

When the clouds of dust thinned there was no sign of anyone—certainly not any dinner for Lion. He went home in a terrible temper, growling like his empty belly.

The next day, Guinea Fowl was at the grassy patch first. You can be sure she had her eyes wide open for Lion.

Soon she saw Cow cautiously crossing the river to join her—shlip, clop, shlop. But something yellow was twitching in the reeds.

Wasn't that Lion's tail?

Up whirred Nganga, half tumbling, half flying with her stubby wings. Lion looked up, startled, from his hiding place. Frrrr . . . a little black whirlwind was racing across the grass toward the river. "Whe-klo-klo-klo!" it called out to Cow.

"Guinea Fowl! That's where the duststorm came from yesterday," growled Lion between his sharp teeth. But the next moment, the whirlwind hit the river.

"RAAUghmf!" Lion exploded with a roar that ended underwater.

"I'll teach that bird to chase away my dinner!" he spluttered. But by the time his roar was working properly again, Cow and Guinea Fowl were safely over the next hill at Cow's house.

"Nganga," mooed Cow gratefully, "twice you have helped me escape from Lion. Now I will help you do the same."

370

Turning around, she dipped her tasseled tail into a calabash of milk. Then she shook the tasselful of milk over Guinea Fowl's sleek black feathers—flick, flock, flick—spattering her with creamy white milk.

Guinea Fowl craned her head and admired the delicate speckles covering her back.

She spread her wings, and Cow sprinkled them with milk too—flick, flock, flick.

"Whe-klo-klo! That's beautiful, Cow!" chuckled Nganga. "Thank you, my friend!"

And she set off for home.

Whom should she meet where the path crossed the river but Lion, still shaking the water out of his ears and angrier than ever.

"Ho, Speckled Bird!" snorted Lion. "Have you seen Guinea Fowl on your path?"

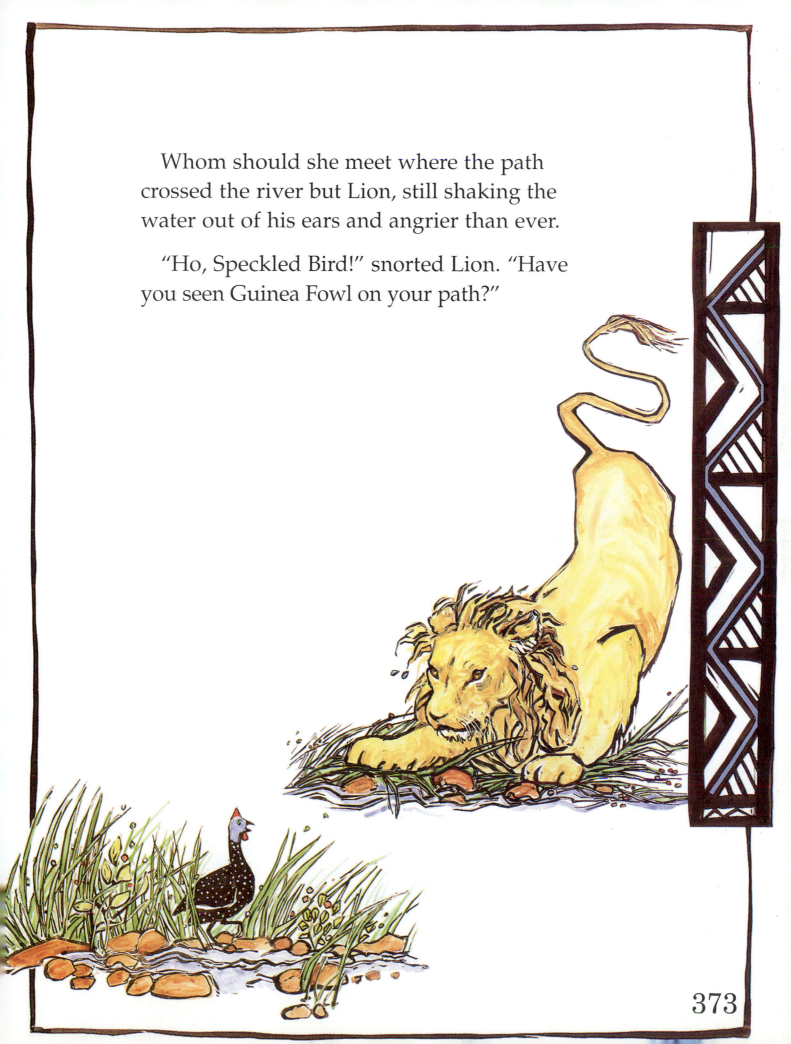

"Oh yes," clucked Nganga, hiding
a smile. "I believe she went that way."

She pointed with her spotted wing to the
hills far down the river.

"If you go quickly and don't stop to rest,
you may catch up with her in a few days."

Lion leaped up at once, not bothering to thank the strange bird. A minute later, he thought about taking her along for a traveling snack, but when he looked back at the riverbank, he could see no trace of her.

"These lovely spots are just the thing for hiding in the shadows and grass!" laughed Nganga, who was, in fact, right where Lion had left her.

And she turned back to Cow's house to thank her friend again.

How the Guinea Fowl Got Her Spots

Meet the Author and Illustrator

Barbara Knutson was born in South Africa. She studied art in Africa and the United States. After receiving a degree in art education and French, she taught English and French in an international school in Nigeria.

Having grown up in South Africa and having traveled in other African countries, Barbara Knutson has a lot of personal experiences to use in her illustrations. Her detailed watercolors show the love and knowledge she has of African culture. She now lives in Minnesota where she visits schools and works at a children's bookstore.

Theme Connections

Think About It

This story tells how one animal was given its camouflage. Discuss the following questions:

- How did Guinea Fowl protect her friend Cow from Lion?
- How did Cow help protect Guinea Fowl?
- What does this selection teach us about animals looking out for one another?
- What does the selection help us to know about camouflage?

Check the Concept/Question Board and answer any questions you can. Post any new questions.

Record Ideas

Write some ways other animals may have been given their camouflage markings.

Make a Chart

- Make a chart to compare what is true in the story to what is just a tale.
- Create two columns. At the top of the left side, write Real Life. At the top of the right side, write Make Believe.
- In the left column list what could happen in real life.
- In the right column list what is make believe.

All Eyes on the Pond

Michael J. Rosen

illustrated by Tom Leonard

Here and there around this pond,
countless eyes watch what goes on.
Listen. They're all calling you:
Come closer, look! Come see my view.

A world of water multiplies
within the eyes of dragonflies,
whose gazes are kaleidoscopes
that spy atop the cattail slopes.

The snapping turtle sometimes sees
the muddy deep, sometimes the trees,
and sometimes nothing but inside
the painted shell where it can hide.

From where the spider always clings
the view is largely tangled things
dangling in the crisscrossed strands
that weave the windows where it stands.

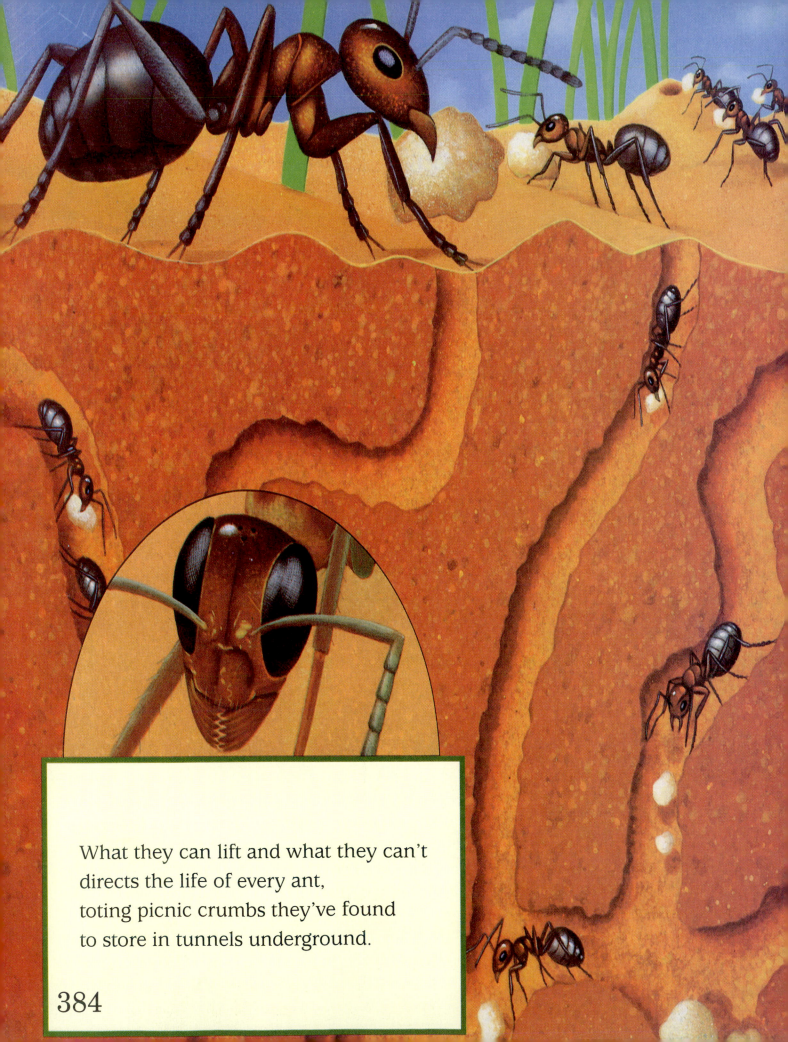

What they can lift and what they can't
directs the life of every ant,
toting picnic crumbs they've found
to store in tunnels underground.

The snail sees simply what it's on
as it glides up a stalk or frond.
Where next? The snail can still decide
as it glides down the other side.

The water strider walks the shine
where air and water form a line.
What's up above? What's down below?
It never has the chance to know.

387

With echoes bouncing through the night,
the bat can see without its sight.
Soundless shadows, hidden prey—
a bat may swoop and snatch away.

To what's ahead, the crawdad's blind.
It only sees what's left behind.
Whooshing backward by its tail,
the crawdad leaves a cloudy trail.

389

Peering toward the breezy air
where clouds are what the branches bear,
the bluegill watches at the brink
the flitting things it hopes will sink.

There . . . beside the fallen log,
the yellow peepers of a frog
who waits beside an old tree trunk,
nabs a fly, and jumps, *kerplunk*.

391

Paddling through the cattail shoots,
lily pads and toppled roots,
a mallard dips and dives and dunks
to munch upon the duckweed clumps.

Chittering swallows skitter so fast
and skim the waves as they soar past,
keeping an eye on all that's afloat—
a branch, a beetle, an anchored boat.

The pond itself, seen from the sky,
appears to be a giant's eye.
What's it watching, staring back?
A storm? The clouds? The zodiac?

If you were here, what would you spy
with your peculiar human eye?
Shhh. Come closer. What's your view?
All the creatures watch for you.

All Eyes on the Pond

Meet the Author

Michael J. Rosen often visited the country with his family when he was a child. He would feed horses, go fishing, and explore the creeks and ponds. In "All Eyes on the Pond," he combines his love of poetry and animals. Before writing the poem, he looked for facts that made each animal different. *"My hope is that anyone who reads "All Eyes on the Pond" will realize that what human eyes see is only one of many viewpoints."*

Meet the Illustrator

Tom Leonard graduated from the Philadelphia College of Art. Before illustrating "All Eyes on the Pond," he visited libraries and ponds to do research. He now lives and works in Pennsylvania.

Theme Connections

Think About It

How do the animals around the pond use camouflage? Here are some questions to discuss:

- How do so many different animals live in and around the same pond together?
- How might the animals around the pond use camouflage to survive?
- Do you think you will see more animals next time you go to a pond? Why?

Check the Concept/Question Board and answer any questions you can.

Record Ideas

Record your thoughts about the questions above in your Writing Journal.

Make a Food Chain

- Think about the animals in the poem and decide which hide to avoid being eaten.
- Diagram a food chain with five animals.
- Begin with an animal that you think is in the most danger of being eaten.
- Decide which animal might eat the first animal. Keep going until you have five animals.
- Your food chain can be a series of pictures or names of animals in a diagram.

Bibliography

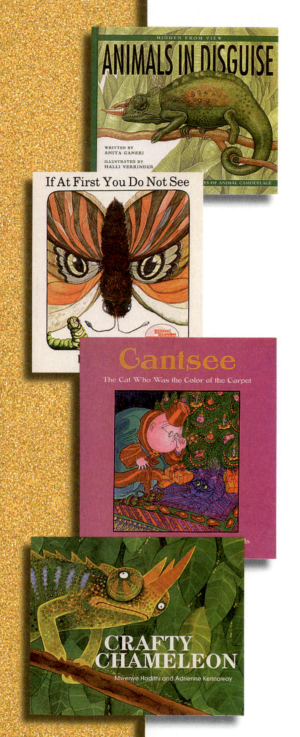

Animals in Disguise

by Anita Ganeri. Sunglasses? False mustaches? Read and find out what animals use for disguises.

If At First You Do Not See

by Ruth Brown. Around the page and upside down, this book is full of surprises. Keep turning and see what you find.

Cantsee: The Cat Who Was the Color of the Carpet

by Gretchen Schields. Mr. Blue wants to give Cantsee, a chameleon-like kitten away. What happens to change his mind?

Crafty Chameleon

by Mwenye Hadithi. How do you handle a bully? Read about the lesson Chameleon teaches Crocodile and Leopard.

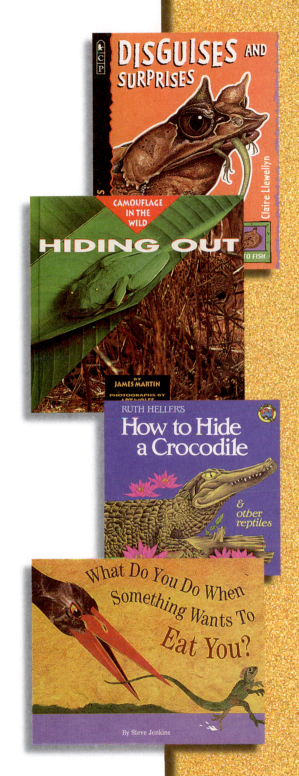

Disguises and Surprises

by Claire Llewellyn. Owls, spiders, polar bears, even flowers have camouflage tricks up their sleeves. Discover what they are!

Hiding Out: Camouflage in the Wild

by James Martin. Hey, what's going on here? Is that an insect or is it a stick? Read and see for yourself.

How to Hide a Crocodile

by Ruth Heller. Even crocodiles need to hide sometimes. Read and find out how they do it!

What Do You Do When Something Wants To Eat You?

by Steve Jenkins. How do 14 different animals escape from becoming someone else's dinner? Guess and read!

Writer's Handbook

Table *of* **C**ontents

Grammar, Mechanics, and Usage

Kinds of Sentences 402

Combining Sentences 403

Parts of a Sentence 404

Ending a Sentence with the Right Mark 405

Using Commas with Lists in a Sentence 406

Using Commas in Dates, Addresses,
   and Letters 407

Using Parentheses 408

Using Capital Letters 409

Kinds of Words (Parts of Speech) and
   How They Are Used 411

Using Nouns That Show Who Owns
   Something 412

Using the Right Pronoun for the Right Noun . . . 414

Using Pronouns That Show Who Owns
   Something 416

Telling About What's Happening Now 418

Telling About What Happened Before 420

Using The Right Verb for the Subject 422

Using Words That Describe
   (Adjectives and Adverbs) 424

Comparing with Adjectives and Adverbs 425

Showing *Where, When,* and *How*
   (Prepositions) 427

Showing That Story Characters Are Talking
   (Dialogue) 429

Study Skills

Parts of a Book 431

Alphabetical Order 433

Using a Dictionary and a Glossary 435

Using an Encyclopedia 437

Using Maps 439

Looking Up Information 441

Finding Books in a Library 443

Understanding and Making a Time Line 445

Understanding and Making a Chart 447

Writing and Technology

Using the Word Processor 449

Using an On-Line Encyclopedia 451

On-Line Safety Tips 453

Grammar, Mechanics, and Usage

Kinds of Sentences

Rule: A **sentence** is a group of words that tells a complete thought. It begins with a capital letter and ends with a punctuation mark.

A sentence can tell about something, ask about something, or show strong feeling about something. Each of these three different kinds of sentences ends with a different punctuation mark.

A sentence that tells about something is called a statement. It ends with a period.

Statement: The dog ran home.

A sentence that asks something is called a question. It ends with a question mark.

Question: Did you see the dog?

A sentence that shows strong feeling about something is called an exclamation. It ends with an exclamation point.

Exclamation: That dog is really fast!

Grammar, Mechanics, and Usage

Combining Sentences

Rule: Two sentences with ideas that are alike can be put together, or combined, by using the word *and*.

You can use the word *and* to combine two sentences if they are about ideas that are alike. Place a comma before the word *and*.

Two Sentences: Rosa walked to the mailbox. She mailed the letter.

Combined Sentence: Rosa walked to the mailbox, and she mailed the letter.

Do not use *and* to combine two sentences that are not about things that are alike. Do not combine these kinds of sentences.

Two Sentences: The letter was for Rosa's friend. Rosa walked home.

Writer's Handbook

Grammar, Mechanics, and Usage

Parts of a Sentence

Rule: A sentence is made up of two parts: a **subject** and a **predicate.** Without these two parts, a group of words is not a complete sentence.

Every sentence has a **subject.** The subject names the person or thing the sentence is about. The subject is underlined in each of these sentences.

> **Subjects:** <u>Jim and Rob</u> are brothers.
>
> <u>Soccer</u> is their favorite sport.
>
> <u>They</u> practice in their backyard.

Every sentence has a **predicate**. The predicate tells what the subject is or does. The predicate is underlined in each of these sentences.

> **Predicates:** Jim and Rob <u>are brothers</u>.
>
> Soccer <u>is their favorite sport</u>.
>
> They <u>practice in their backyard</u>.

Grammar, Mechanics, and Usage

Ending a Sentence with the Right Mark

Rule: End every sentence with a punctuation mark: a period, a question mark, or an exclamation point. Use different end marks for different kinds of sentences.

If a sentence tells about something, it is a statement. End a statement with **period (.)**.

> **Statement:** José has a new puppy.

If a sentence asks something, it is a question. End a question with a **question mark (?)**.

> **Question:** Can you hear the puppy bark?

If a sentence shows strong feeling, it is an exclamation. End an exclamation with an **exclamation mark (!)**.

> **Exclamation:** It's such a loud puppy!

Using Commas with Lists in a Sentence

Rule: In a list of three or more things of the same type, put a comma after each word that comes before *and* or *or*.

In a list of three or more persons, places, or things, use a comma after each word that comes before *and* or *or*.

> **Things:** Frogs eat <u>bugs</u>, <u>worms</u>, and <u>spiders</u>.

In a list of three or more descriptive words, use a comma after each word that comes before *and* or *or*.

> **Descriptive Words:** The bullfrog is <u>large</u>, <u>green</u>, and <u>powerful</u>.

In a list of three or more action words, use a comma after each word that comes before *and* or *or*.

> **Action Words:** The frogs <u>croak</u>, <u>leap</u>, or <u>hop</u> about.

Grammar, Mechanics, and Usage

Using Commas in Dates, Addresses, and Letters

Rule: Use commas in dates, in addresses when names of places are used, and in letters.

In dates, use a comma between the day and the year.

> **Dates:** My Aunt Maria was born March 17, 1973.
>
> Her baby was born June 29, 1992.

In addresses, use a comma between the parts of a place name.

> **Addresses:** Aunt Maria now lives in Dallas, Texas.
>
> Her baby was born in Richmond, Virginia.

In a friendly letter, use a comma after the greeting, or words you use to say hello, and in the closing, the words you use to say good-bye.

> **Greeting:** Dear Aunt Maria,
>
> **Closing:** Love,

Writer's Handbook

Grammar, Mechanics, and Usage

Using Parentheses

Rule: Parentheses are punctuation marks. Use parentheses to show information that is added to the sentence.

Put parentheses around extra information in a sentence. The information may tell what one of the words in the sentence means. It may also tell the reader more about another part of the sentence.

Extra information about the meaning of one of the words:

Ralphie is a canine (dog).

Extra information about the idea in the sentence:

Columbus's first voyage to North America (1492) was an important event.

Grammar, Mechanics, and Usage

Using Capital Letters

Rule: Always capitalize the first word in a sentence. Always capitalize the word *I*. Capitalize other words only if they are used in a special way.

Begin the first word of a sentence with a capital letter.

First Word: <u>Today</u> the circus comes to town.
<u>My</u> family will go to the circus.

Write the word *I* with a capital letter.

The Word *I*: Will I see lions and tigers?
My sister and I also like the clowns.

Begin names of people and places with capital letters.

People and Places: Dr. Jane R. Smith
Uncle Al   Fifth Avenue   Indian Ocean

Begin the days of the week and months of the year with capital letters.

Days of the Week: Friday   Tuesday
Months of the Year: August 10
the week of May 19

Grammar, Mechanics, and Usage
Using Capital Letters (continued)

Do <u>not</u> begin the seasons of the year with capital letters unless they are the first words of sentences.

winter   spring   summer   autumn   fall

Capitalize words used to show directions only when they are part of the name of a place or the name of a street.

Directions Capitalized:
West Park Street   North Dakota

Directions Not Capitalized:
one block west   north of here

Grammar, Mechanics, and Usage

Kinds of Words (Parts of Speech) and How They Are Used

Rule: Language is made up of different kinds of words. They include **nouns, pronouns, verbs, adjectives,** and **adverbs.**

A **noun** names a person, place, or thing.

Nouns: Alice sings happy songs.

A **pronoun** takes the place of a noun.

Pronoun: Alice sings happy songs.
She is a singer.

A **verb** names an action or tells what someone or something is, was, or will be.

Verbs: Alice sings happy songs.
She is a singer.

An **adjective** describes a noun or a pronoun.

Adjectives: Alice is a good singer.
She is talented.

An **adverb** can describe a verb. It may answer the questions *How? How often? When?* or *Where?*

Adverbs: Alice sings happily.
She sang two songs today.

Writer's Handbook

Grammar, Mechanics, and Usage

Using Nouns That Show Who Owns Something

Rule: A **possessive noun** is a word that names a person, place, or thing that owns or has something. Possessive nouns are singular or plural.

A singular noun names one person, place, or thing. To make a singular noun possessive, add an apostrophe and an *s ('s)*.

Singular Noun: <u>Maria</u> has two birds.

Possessive Noun: <u>Maria's</u> birds are green.

A plural noun names more than one person, place, or thing. Most plural nouns end with *s*. To make a plural noun ending in *s* possessive, just add an apostrophe after the *s (s')*.

Plural Noun Ending with *s*: The <u>girls</u> own two bikes.

Possessive Noun: The <u>girls'</u> bikes are new.

Grammar, Mechanics, and Usage

Using Nouns That Show Who Owns Something (continued)

If a plural noun does not end with *s*, add an apostrophe and *s (*'s)* just as for the singular form.

Plural Noun Not Ending with *s:*
The <u>children</u> have books on the table.

Possessive Noun: The <u>children's</u> books are on the table.

Grammar, Mechanics, and Usage

Using the Right Pronoun for the Right Noun

Rule: **Pronouns** are words that take the place of nouns. Use pronouns that agree in number with the nouns that they replace.

Singular pronouns stand for one person or thing. Use singular pronouns to take the place of singular nouns.

Singular Nouns and Pronouns:
<u>Ann</u> got a new <u>baseball</u>.
<u>She</u> threw <u>it</u> far.

Plural pronouns stand for more than one person or thing. Use plural pronouns to take the place of plural nouns.

Plural Nouns and Pronouns:
The <u>children</u> were playing.
<u>They</u> played ball.

Grammar, Mechanics, and Usage

**Using the Right Pronoun for
the Right Noun (continued)**

This chart shows some pronouns you use
often:

Singular Pronouns	Plural Pronouns
I, me	we, us
you	you
he, she, him, her, it	they, them

Be sure your readers know exactly to whom
or what each pronoun refers. If it is not clear
to which noun a pronoun refers, use the
nouns again.

Not Clear: Kate showed Mary her new
coat. She really liked it. (Does
she refer to Kate or to Mary?)

Clear: Kate showed Mary her new coat.
Mary really liked it.

Writer's Handbook

Grammar, Mechanics, and Usage

Using Pronouns That Show Who Owns Something

Rule: A pronoun is a word that takes the place of a noun. It is a word that stands for a person, place, or thing. Use a **possessive pronoun** to show who owns or has something.

Use a possessive pronoun in place of a possessive noun. Here is a list of pronouns that show who owns something:

my, your, his, her, its, our, their

Possessive Noun: The <u>boy's</u> dog ran into the street.

Possessive Pronoun: <u>His</u> dog ran into the street.
(His stands for boy's.)

Possessive Noun: The <u>children's</u> pets played outside.

Possessive Pronoun: <u>Their</u> pets played outside.
(Their stands for children's.)

Grammar, Mechanics, and Usage

Using Pronouns That Show Who Owns Something (continued)

Do not mix up the pronoun *its* with the word *it's*. *It's* means "it is."

> **Not a Possessive Pronoun:** It's fun to read that book.
>
> **Possessive Pronoun:** Its pictures are pretty.

Do not mix up the pronoun *your* with the word *you're*. *You're* means "you are."

> **Not a Possessive Pronoun:** You're writing a story.
>
> **Possessive Pronoun:** Your story is about a circus.

Grammar, Mechanics, and Usage

Telling About What's Happening Now

Rule: Verbs in the **present tense** show action that is happening now. These verbs can also show action that happens again and again.

If the subject of a sentence is singular (only one person, place, or thing), add -*s* to the verb to put it in the present tense. This rule works for most verbs.

> **Add -*s*:** David <u>walks</u> home from school. He <u>climbs</u> the steps to his house. The cat <u>greets</u> David.

Some verbs have special rules for telling what is happening now. If the verb ends with *ch*, *sh*, *s*, *x*, or *z*, add -*es* to a verb that is used with a singular subject.

> **Add -*es*:** David <u>fixes</u> a snack. The cat <u>watches</u> him.

If the verb ends with a consonant followed by *y*, change the *y* to *i* and add -*es*.

> **Change *y* to *i* and Add -*es*:** He <u>hurries</u> across the street.

Grammar, Mechanics, and Usage

Telling About What's Happening Now (continued)

If the subject of a sentence is *I* or *you*, do not add an ending to the verb. Do not add an ending if the subject is plural (more than one).

> **No Ending:** I <u>like</u> a bus. You <u>ride</u> in the car. Boys <u>walk</u> with him. They <u>climb</u> the steps.

Some present-tense verbs have different forms. Pay special attention to them when you write.

Verb	Present-Tense Forms
be	I <u>am</u>. You <u>are</u>. We <u>are</u>. They <u>are</u>. He <u>is</u>. She <u>is</u>. It <u>is</u>.
have	I <u>have</u>. We <u>have</u>. You <u>have</u>. They <u>have</u>. He <u>has</u>. She <u>has</u>. It <u>has</u>.

Grammar, Mechanics, and Usage

Telling About What Happened Before

Rule: Verbs in the **past tense** show action that has already happened.

You can add *-ed* to many verbs to put them in the past tense.

Add *-ed:* Kelly <u>painted</u> a picture. She <u>liked</u> it. She <u>carried</u> it to the kitchen. She <u>showed</u> it to Mom.

You must sometimes follow special rules when you add *-ed* to verbs. If the verb ends with *e*, drop *e* when you add *-ed*.

Drop *-e:* She <u>liked</u> it.

If the verb ends with a consonant followed by *y*, change the *y* to *i* and add *-ed*.

Change *y* to *i* and Add *-ed:* She <u>carried</u> it to the kitchen.

For most verbs that have one syllable, one short vowel, and one final consonant, double that final consonant before adding *-ed*.

Double Final Consonant: Mother <u>stopped</u>. She <u>plugged</u> in the iron.

Grammar, Mechanics, and Usage

Telling About What Happened Before (continued)

Some past-tense verbs have special forms. Here are some common examples.

Verb	Past-Tense Forms
be	was, were
do	did
have	had
go	went
come	came
say	said
give	gave

Writer's Handbook

Grammar, Mechanics, and Usage

Using the Right Verb for the Subject

Rule: In a sentence, the verb must **agree** with the subject. A singular subject (only one) takes a singular verb. A plural subject (more than one) takes a plural verb.

The **subject** of a sentence is the word or words that refer to the person or thing that does the action of the verb. The **verb** is the word that refers to the action.

Most verbs follow this pattern in the present tense:

Present Tense	
Singular	*Plural*
I work	we work
you work	you work
he, she, it works	they work

Notice that for all subjects except *he*, *she*, or *it*, the verb is the same.

Grammar, Mechanics, and Usage

**Using the Right Verb for
the Subject (continued)**

For *he*, *she*, or *it*, and for all subjects that
can be referred to as *he*, *she*, or *it*, the verb
usually takes the ending -*s*.

> **Subject can be referred to as *he*:**
> Pepe plays soccer.

Verbs that end in -*s*, -*x*, -*ch*, or -*sh* take the
ending -*es*.

> **Verb ends in -*ch*:** The goalie touches the
> ball with his hands.

In verbs that end in a consonant plus *y*, the *y*
changes to *i* before the -*es* ending.

> **Verb ends in consonant plus *y*:**
> The baby cries when she is hungry.

Grammar, Mechanics, and Usage

Using Words That Describe (Adjectives and Adverbs)

Rule: An **adjective** is a describing word. Use an adjective to describe a person, place, or thing. An adverb is also a describing word. Use an adverb to tell something about the action in a sentence. An **adverb** can tell when, where, how, or how often the action happened.

An **adjective** describes a person, a place, or a thing.

> **Adjectives:** Marcie found a gold ring.
> The ring was in the old house.

An **adverb** can tell about the action of the sentence. Adverbs tell where, when, how, or how often.

> **Adverbs:** Marcie held the ring carefully.
> (tells how)
> She took it outside. (tells where)

Many adverbs end in *-ly*.

> **Adverb:** Marcie walked quickly.
> (quick + *-ly*)

Comparing with Adjectives and Adverbs

Rule: **Adjectives** and **adverbs** are describing words. Adjectives are used to describe people, places, and things. Adverbs are used to describe actions. You can use adjectives and adverbs to compare.

If the adjective has one or two syllables, add the -*er* ending to compare two things. Add the -*est* ending to compare more than two.

Examples: soft   softer   (the) softest

No Comparison: This puppy has soft fur.
Comparing Two: The kitten has softer fur than the puppy.

Comparing More Than Two: The baby hamster has the softest fur of all.

If the adjective has more than two syllables, use the word *more* to compare two things. Use the word *most* to compare more than two. When you use *more* or *most*, do not add an -*er* or -*est* ending.

Examples: powerful   more powerful (the) most powerful

Grammar, Mechanics, and Usage

Comparing with Adjectives and Adverbs (continued)

Usually, adverbs end in the letters *-ly*. Before adverbs ending in *-ly*, use *more* to compare two actions. Use *most* to compare more than two.

Examples:
quickly   more quickly   (the) most quickly

No Comparison:	Lee works <u>quickly</u>.
Comparing Two:	Tim works <u>more quickly</u> than Lee.
Comparing More Than Two:	Alan works the <u>most quickly</u> of all.

A few adverbs do not end in *-ly*. To these adverbs, add the ending *-er* to compare two actions. Add the ending *-est* to compare more than two.

Examples:
hard   harder   (the) hardest

The spelling of an adjective or an adverb may change when you add the ending *-er* or *-est*.

Examples: big   bigger   (the) biggest

Writer's Handbook

Grammar, Mechanics, and Usage

Showing Where, When, and How (Prepositions)

Rule: Some words are used to show where something is. Other words help show when or how something happened. These words are called **prepositions.** Prepositions are not used alone.

Prepositions are used with nouns. The nouns usually come after the preposition.

Prepositions:

in the house   around the corner

after lunch   from Pat

A preposition can show **where** something is or where something happens.

Where: The bag is on the table.

Jacob reached into the bag.

A preposition can show **when** something happens or happened.

When: I saw Brianna after school.

Grammar, Mechanics, and Usage

Showing Where, When, and How (continued)

Some prepositions tell **how** something happens or happened.

How: Larry cut the paper <u>with</u> scissors.

Here are some prepositions you can use in your writing. Use prepositions with nouns.

above	before	during	to
after	behind	in	until
around	by	near	with

Writer's Handbook

Grammar, Mechanics, and Usage

Showing That Story Characters Are Talking (Dialogue)

Rule: In a story, what characters say to each other is called **dialogue.** A speaker's exact words are called a quotation. These words are put inside quotation marks (" ").

Place quotation marks (" ") before and after a speaker's exact words.

Quotation Marks:

"It's a beautiful day," said Brian.

Begin the first word of a quotation with a capital letter, even if it is not at the beginning of a sentence.

Capital Letters:

"Let's go back to the beach," said Kim.
Brian said, "We can't go to the beach today."

Use a comma to separate a quotation from the rest of the sentence.

Commas:

"The beach would be fun," said Kim.
Brian replied, "But today is a school day."

Grammar, Mechanics, and Usage

**Showing That Story Characters
Are Talking (Dialogue) (continued)**

Words such as *said Kim* tell who is
speaking. They are called speaker tags.

Put the end mark for the quotation inside the
closing quotation marks.

End Marks:
Kim snapped, "Let's check a calendar."
"Go ahead and check," said Brian.
"Yes, it's a beach day!" Kim exclaimed.
"Are you joking?" asked Brian.

Writer's Handbook

Study Skills

Parts of a Book

All books have a **title page** and a **copyright page.** Some books also have a **table of contents, glossary,** and **index.**

You don't always have to read a whole book to find information. Use the parts of a book to find only the information you need. The parts of a book can help you find out what the book is about, the page on which stories or articles begin, and the meaning of new words.

The **title page** is usually the first printed page at the front of the book. It gives

- the title
- the name of the author or editor
- the name of the publisher

The **copyright** comes after the title page. It gives

- the publisher's name
- the place and year the book was published

The **table of contents** is a list of each unit, story, or chapter in the book and the number of the page on which each begins.

Study Skills
Parts of a Book (continued)

The **glossary** is a list of new or special words used in the book. It has

- words, their definitions, and sometimes their pronunciations, listed in ABC order

The **index** is a list of names, places, and topics found in the book. It has

- names, places, and topics, listed in ABC order
- page numbers for each mention of the name, place, or topic

Writer's Handbook

Study Skills

Alphabetical Order

Alphabetical order, or **ABC order**, means that the words are put in the same order as the letters of the alphabet. When you put words in ABC order, think about the order of the letters of the alphabet.

The words in dictionaries, encyclopedias, card catalogs, indexes, and glossaries are listed in ABC order. Knowing the rules for ABC order will help you find and list information more easily.

- When words start with different letters, use the first letter of each word to put the words in ABC order.

  Start with Different Letters:

  cat   horse   lion

- When words have the same first letter, use the next letter that is different in each word to put the words in ABC order.

  Start with Same Letter:

  deer   dog   duck

- If *a*, *an*, or *the* is the first word of a title, do not use it. Instead, use the first letter of the second word.

Study Skills

Alphabetical Order (continued)

Start with *A*, *An*, or *The*:
The Empty Pot
A Pair of Red Clogs
The Tale of Peter Rabbit

- When you look up or list names, use the first letter of the person's last name. Often people's names are listed with the last name first.

  Last Name First: Lobel, Arnold
  Matsumo, Masako
  Yashima, Taro

Writer's Handbook

Study Skills

Using a Dictionary or Glossary

A **dictionary** is a book that gives meanings for the words you use every day when you speak, write, or read. A **glossary** is the part of a book that gives the meaning of words you find in that book.

- The words in a dictionary or glossary are listed in ABC order. They are also printed in dark type. These words are called **entry words.** If you were looking for the entry word *feast*, you would look for the letter *f*.

- At the top of each page of a dictionary are two words called **guide words.** Guide words show the first and last entry words on that page. Only entry words that come between those two words in ABC order will be found on that page. For example, *feast* would come between the guide words *entry* and *generous*.

Study Skills
Using a Dictionary or Glossary (continued)

Use dictionaries and glossaries to find the meanings of new words you read. Check words in a dictionary when you proofread your own writing. This is what an entry for *feast* might look in a dictionary or glossary.

> **feast** (fēst) *v.* to eat very well; to eat a lot of good food. —*n.* A large, fancy meal.

- The information in the entry tells how the word is pronounced (fēst), what part of speech it is (*v.* and *n.*), and what meanings the word has.

A dictionary entry for a word tells much more about the word than a glossary entry does. A glossary entry tells only the meaning of the word as it is used in that book.

Writer's Handbook

Study Skills

Using an Encyclopedia

An **encyclopedia** is one or more books that contain information on many subjects. Each book in a set is called a volume. The subjects within are usually arranged in ABC order. Each volume is marked to show what subjects are inside. Some encyclopedias use numbers as marks; others use letters. In a set, one volume is usually an index.

An encyclopedia is a good place to find information about a subject. To use it, follow these guidelines.

- Think about your subject. What is the most important word in your subject? For example, if you want to find out how the pilgrims lived, *pilgrims* is the most important word. If your subject is a person, look for information under the person's last name.

   Examples: Pilgrims   Washington, George

Study Skills

Using an Encyclopedia (continued)

- If your encyclopedia has an index, look up the word there. Next to the word you look up, you will see a volume number or letter, a colon (:), and a page number.

  Examples: Washington, George 23:95
  (or W:19)

  This tells you that there is an article about George Washington in volume 23, beginning on page 95 (or in volume W, beginning on page 19).

- Find the volume you need, then turn to the page. Read through the article and take notes on the most important information about your subject.

- At the end of the article, you may see a list of other articles in the encyclopedia. These articles may have more information about your subject.

  Example: *See also* **Mount Vernon; Revolutionary War.**

Writer's Handbook

Study Skills

Using Maps

Maps are drawings that show where places and things, such as rivers, mountains, cities, roads, parks, and buildings, can be found. A book of maps is called an **atlas.** A **globe** shows the round shape of the world and has on it a map of the Earth.

On a map, lines, colors, and pictures are used to show things. Here are some guidelines for using maps.

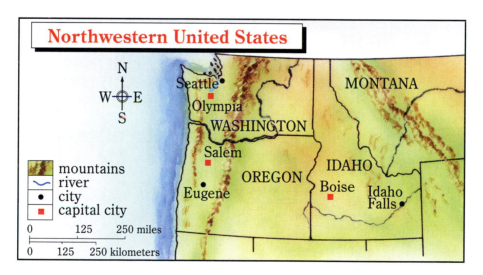

- Read the **title.** The title of a map tells what the map shows. This map is a map of the northwestern United States.

Study Skills

Using Maps (continued)

- Find the **map key.** The map key shows the special pictures, lines, and colors that are used on the map. Here are the pictures that are used for the map on page 439.

| | mountains | ● | city |
| | river | ■ | capital city |

- Look at the **direction arrows.** These show north, south, east, and west on the map. North is usually toward the top of the map. This means that south is toward the bottom, east is to the right, and west is to the left.

- Use the map key and direction arrows to find out about the places on the map. For example, this map shows that Olympia is the capital city of Washington. It is located north of Salem.

Writer's Handbook

Study Skills

Looking Up Information

There are many ways to find information. You can find it by reading, talking to people, or visiting museums. You will spend less time looking for facts if you know where to look.

When you are doing research, decide where the best place is to find the kinds of facts you need. Here are some places to find information.

- An **atlas** is a book of maps. Use an atlas if you need to find out about a continent, country, state, or city. You can also find out about oceans, rivers, or mountains.

- A **dictionary** is a book that lists words in ABC order. Use a dictionary if you need to find the spellings and meanings of words and how to say them.

- An **encyclopedia** is a set of books that contains facts on many subjects. The subjects are in ABC order. You can find many useful facts in an encyclopedia article.

Study Skills

Looking Up Information (continued)

- **Magazines** and **newspapers** contain many facts. You can get the most up-to-date information from them.

- A **nonfiction book** presents facts on a topic. You may read the whole book for information, or you may take facts from a few pages of the book.

- An **interview** means talking with someone and asking questions to find out facts.

- A **museum** can give facts on a special subject. A museum has exhibits and books. At a museum, you can also talk to people who know about a subject.

Writer's Handbook

Study Skills

Finding Books in a Library

Each library has a **catalog**—a list of all the books in a library. The catalog lists each book three ways: by the author's name, by the title of the book, and by the subject of the book.

The catalog helps you quickly find books in your library. It is a good place to start your research. To find books in a library, you should know the following information:

- The catalog may be on cards or on a computer. If it is on cards, small file drawers hold the cards in ABC order. If it is on a computer, the catalog will contain the same kind of information that the cards contain.

- The catalog has three types of cards or ways to look for a book. An **author** card is filed by the author's name, last name first. A **title** card is filed by the book's title. A **subject** card is filed by the subject of the book. You can look up an author's name, a book title, or a subject.

Study Skills

Finding Books in a Library (continued)

- The entry for a book contains a **call number.** This number helps you find which shelf the book belongs on.

- The entry names the **publisher,** the company that made the book. It also shows where and when the book was made.

- The entry tells how many pages the book has and whether it has pictures.

- An entry often tells what the book is about. You can use the summary to help you decide whether the book has the information you need.

Study Skills

Understanding and Making a Time Line

A **time line** shows the order in which important events happened over a specific period of time. It can help readers understand important facts. A time line may be as long or as short as it needs to be. It may cover one year, a hundred years, or thousands of years.

Making a time line can help you present important facts from your research. Here are guidelines for making a time line.

- Decide what you want to show in your time line. Choose a title for it.
  Example: How My Plant Grew

- Make a list of the main events and the time of each one. Use short phrases.
  Examples: Planted seed—March
  Sprout came up—April
  Leaves came out—May
  Plant bloomed—June

- Draw a line across a sheet of paper. Above and below the line, leave space for writing the events and the times—in order, going from left to right.

Study Skills

Understanding and Making a Time Line (continued)

- On the line, make a dot for the time of each event. Make the space between the dots different, according to the length of time between events.

- Below each dot, write a time.

- Above each dot, write an event.

Planted seed	Sprout came up	Leaves came out	Plant bloomed
●	●	●	●
March	April	May	June

Writer's Handbook

Study Skills

Understanding and Making a Chart

A **chart** can show a lot of information in a little space. Words or numbers are written in boxes to help readers find information quickly.

Many books and magazines use charts. You can use them in your own writing. Then you can show a lot of information clearly. The following information will help you understand and make charts.

- A chart shows the same kind of information about several different things. For example, a chart might show information about some different vegetables: their colors, their shapes, and which part of the plant they are.

Vegetables			
Name	*Color*	*Shape*	*Part*
peas	green	round	seeds
carrots	orange	long, thin	roots
beets	reddish	round	roots

Study Skills

Understanding and Making a Chart (continued)

- A chart has a title that tells what it is about.

- Headings across the top of the chart tell what kinds of information will be shown about each thing.

- Headings that are written down the left side of the chart show what things will be described.

- Lines make the chart easy to read. The lines make boxes.

- Words or numbers—not sentences—are inside the boxes.

Writer's Handbook

Writing and Technology

Using a Word Processor

A **word processor** is a special kind of computer program. It is a program that helps you create, edit, save, and print written works.

There are many types of word processors. Each looks a little different from the others. However, almost all word processing programs allow you to do certain tasks. These tasks include the following:

- You can start a **new** piece of writing. You will then see a blank white part of the screen. In most programs, do this by selecting the command NEW on the FILE menu.

- You can work on an existing piece of writing. To do this, you **open** a file that was made at an earlier time. In most programs, do this by selecting the command OPEN on the FILE menu.

- You can type text. Just click on the white screen and start to **type.**

- You can change or **edit** text. To add words, click on the place where you want the words. Then type them. To take out words, first select them with the mouse. Then tap the delete or backspace (⇐) key.

Writing and Technology

Using a Word Processor (continued)

- You can **save** your work on a disk or on the computer. In most programs, do this by selecting the command SAVE on the FILE menu.

- You can **print** your work. In most programs, do this by selecting the command PRINT on the FILE menu.

Writer's Handbook

Writing and Technology

Using an On-Line Encyclopedia

An **on-line encyclopedia** contains information on many subjects. The subjects within it are usually arranged in ABC order. An on-line encyclopedia is a good place to find information about a number of subjects.

Most encyclopedias use **search tools.** These are programs that find information. There are different kinds of search tools, but these guidelines will help you use most of them:

- Think about your subject. What is the most important word in your subject? For example, if you want to find out when Texas became a state, *Texas* is the most important word. If your subject is a person, look for information under the person's last name.
  Examples: Texas   O'Keeffe, Georgia

- Type a word or short phrase into the empty box on the search tool screen. Make sure that your spelling is correct. Then click SEARCH or FIND.

- You will usually see a list of articles that contain the word or phrase you typed. Click on any title that you want to read.

Using an On-Line Encyclopedia (continued)

- If you do not get a list of articles, try using a different word. For example, if the word *painter* does not work, try *artist*.

- If you get a list of articles that is very long, try adding another word to the box on the search tool. For example, instead of *government*, try *state government*.

- Often, an article will contain links to related articles. A link looks like an underlined word or phrase. Often it is a different color from the other text. When you click on a link, a new article or screen will appear.

- Use the BACK button or arrow (⇐) to return to a screen that you saw earlier.

Many on-line encyclopedias allow you to print articles. This is useful because it allows you to read articles later, when you are not using the computer.

Writer's Handbook

Writing and Technology

On-Line Safety Tips

Computers can connect you to the whole world. Many people use computers to communicate with others on-line. They communicate by E-mail and by meeting in areas called chat rooms.

You can have fun meeting people on-line. You can also learn about different places. However, when you meet people on-line, you need to follow certain safety rules.

- Never believe everything you read on-line. Remember that many people make up things about themselves on-line. For example, they might pretend to be older or younger than they really are. They may pretend to have another name.

- Never give out personal information on-line. Do not give your whole name or your address. Do not give your phone number or the name of your school. If someone asks for this information, tell an adult.

- Never give out your password. Do not even tell it to your friends.

Writing and Technology

On-Line Safety Tips (continued)

- Never agree to meet anyone in person unless you first tell an adult. Make sure to get the adult's permission.

- Never send a picture of yourself to someone you don't know. If someone asks for a picture, check with an adult.

Safety rules are important. In person, you know that you should be careful about strangers. On-line, you should follow the same rules.

Glossary

A

accept (ik sept´) *v.* To like and use.

admire (ad mīr´) *v.* To be pleased with.

adobe (ə dō´ bē) *n.* A building made of brick or dried mud.

adventure (əd ven´ chər) *n.* A task or event that is likely to be exciting or dangerous.

amazement (ə māz´ mənt) *n.* Being very surprised and full of wonder.

amazing (ə mā´ zing) *adj.* Surprising; causing wonder.

amid (ə mid´) *prep.* In with; around; in the middle of.

anemone (ə ne´ mə nē) *n.* A sea animal that looks like a flower.

anole (ə nō´ lē) *n.* A lizard.

Apache (ə pa´ chē) *adj.* Pertaining to a Native American group of the southwestern United States.

Appalachian Mountains (a´ pə lā´ shən moun´ tənz) *n.* A mountain range in the eastern part of the United States.

457

assistant (ə sis′ tənt) *n.* A helper; a person whose job is to help another person.

assure (ə shûr′) *v.* To make sure.

available (ə vā′ lə bəl) *adj.* Being in the area and ready to use.

B

balkity (bô′ kə dē) *adj.* Not willing to move.

ball (bôl) *n.* A large, fancy party at which people dance.

bear (bâr) *v.* To hold up; to carry.

beard (bērd) *n.* Hair on a chin.

bide (bīd) *v.* To wait.

bloom (blōōm) *n.* A large group of plankton on the ocean surface.

blubber (blu′ bər) *n.* Fat found on whales and other large sea animals.

brink (bringk) *n.* Edge.

bristle (bri′ səl) *v.* To stick up stiffly; to be thickly covered by something that looks like bristles.

brow (brou) *n.* Area including the eyebrows and forehead.

bulletin board (bu′ lə tən bord) *n.* A place on a wall for messages and other information.

burr (bûr) *n.* A fruit from a weed that has a bristly outside that easily sticks to fur, hair, or clothing.

burrow (bûr′ ō′) *n.* A hole made in the ground where an animal, such as a rabbit, lives.

C

calabash (ka′ lə bash′) *n.* A gourd with a hard shell that can be made into a dipper.

camouflage (kam′ ə fläzh) *n.* A color or pattern that helps an animal blend into its surroundings.

cane (kān) *n.* A stick to help a person in walking.

capture (kap′ chər) *v.* To catch and hold.

cattail (kat′ tāl′) *n.* A tall reedy plant with a fuzzy brown top that grows in very wet areas.

cautiously (kô′ shəs lē) *adv.* With care; watching out for danger.

cave dweller (kāv dwe′ lər) *n.* A person who lives in a cave.

ceiling (sē′ ling) *n.* The top of a room.

cellar (sel′ ər) *n.* A room underground.

chance (chans) *n.* A time for one to do something.

character (kar′ ik tər) *n.* A mark or symbol used in writing.

chatter (cha′ tər) *v.* To click together quickly.

cinder (sin′ dər) *n.* A small bit of coal or wood that has been burned until it is black.

clearing (klēr′ ing) *n.* In a forest, a piece of land with no trees or bushes.

clearing

clever (kle′ vər) *adj.* Very smart.

coachman (kōch′ mən) *n.* A person who drives a carriage.

cobbler (kob′ lər) *n.* A person who makes and repairs shoes.

coloration (kə′ lə rā′ shən) *n.* The way something is colored.

communicate (kə myoo′ ni kāt′) *v.* To exchange or share knowledge or information.

concentration (kon′ sən trā′ shən) *n.* The act of thinking about one thing or purpose.

concrete torpedo (kon′ krēt tor pē′ dō) *n.* A heavy block of stone used to hit something hard enough to make it break apart.

confuse (kən fyooz′) *v.* To make someone or something unsure.

constitution (kon′ sti too′ shən) *n.* A written document that tells the laws or rules of a group of people.

costume (kos′ toom′) *n.* Something put on to change the way one looks.

cot (kot) *n.* A small bed that usually can be folded.

countless (kount´ ləs) *adj*. Too many to count; very many.

crane (krān) *n*. A bird with a long neck, beak, and legs that lives near water.

crept (krept) *v*. A past tense of **creep:** To move slowly and quietly.

crew (krōō) *n*. A group of people who work together.

crumpled (krum´ pəld) *adj.* Crushed and bent out of shape.

culture (kul´ chər) *n*. The arts, beliefs, and way of life of a group of people.

D

dapple (da´ pəl) *v*. To color with spots of light and shadow.

decorate (de´ kə rāt´) *v*. To add designs or pictures to make something look better.

den (den) *n*. A home for a wild animal.

department (di pärt´ mənt) *n*. A single area of a store; a part of a store where one type of item is sold.

disguise (də skīz´) *n*. Something worn to make one look different or to help one hide. *v*. To cover with something to hide.

down (doun) *n*. Soft feathers.

dreamt (dremt) *v*. The past tense of **dream:** To think of things during sleep.

drenched (drencht) *adj.* Wet all the way through; soaked.

dusk (dusk) *n*. The time just before dark.

E

eager (ē´ gər) *adj.* Looking forward to doing something.

elves (elvz) *n*. The plural of **elf:** A small fairy who sometimes plays tricks.

enormous (i nôr´ məs) *adj.* Huge; very big.

escalator (es´ kə lā´ tər) *n.* A moving stairway.

exclaim (iks klām´) *v.* To cry out suddenly.

F

fawn (fôn) *n.* A young deer.

fix (fiks) *v.* To set; to plan to do.

flick (flik) *v.* To move in a rapid or jerky way.

flitting (fli´ ting) *adj.* Moving quickly and lightly.

forgave (fər gāv´) *v.* The past tense of **forgive**: To pardon; to excuse.

frilly (fri´ lē) *adj.* Being very fancy.

frond (frond) *n.* A large leaf.

froth (frôth) *n.* Bubbles formed in a liquid; foamy liquid.

G

gasp (gasp) *v.* To breathe in gulps with the mouth wide open.

gaze (gāz) *n.* A look at something for a long time.

giddy (gi´ dē) *adj.* Silly.

glare (glâr) *v.* To look at with anger.

glisten (gli´ sən) *v.* To shine or sparkle.

glossy (glo´ sē) *adj.* Having a shine or luster.

gown (goun) *n.* A woman's dress, often fancy.

granary (grā´ nə rē) *n.* A building in which grains, such as corn or wheat, are stored.

guinea fowl (gi´ nē foul) *n.* An African bird that has a bare neck and head.

guinea fowl

gulp (gulp) *n.* To swallow large amounts of something all at one time.

H

herd (hûrd) *n.* A group of animals.

hereabouts (hēr´ ə bouts) *adv.* Around here; nearby.

honor (on´ ər) *v.* To show great respect.

host (hōst) *n.* The person who is taking care of guests.

hover (hu´ vər) *v.* To stay in one place while in the air.

howl (houl) *v.* To cry or shout out loudly.

huddle (hud´ l) *v.* To crowd together; to wrap up tightly in.

I

ice-breaker (īs´ brā´ kər) *n.* A ship used to break a channel through ice.

ice-breaker

ice-pole (īs´ pōl) *n.* A metal pole with a pointed end used to chip ice.

imitator (i´ mə tā´ tər) *n.* One who copies something or someone.

interpreter (in tûr´ pri tər) *n.* A person who can translate statements from one language to another.

Inuit (i´ nŏŏ wət) *n.* People native to the northwestern part of North America and Arctic.

invincible (in´ vin´ sə bəl) *adj.* So strong that it cannot be beaten or broken.

K

kaleidoscope (kə lī′ də skōp′) *n.* A constantly changing pattern or scene.

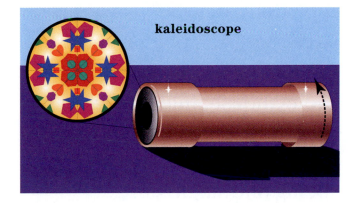

kaleidoscope

L

lad (lad) *n.* A male child; boy.

lap (lap) *v.* To drink by pulling liquid into the mouth with the tongue.

lean (lēn) *v.* To sit with one's back resting against something.

leapt (lept) *v.* The past tense of **leap:** To jump.

leather (leth′ ər) *n.* The skin of an animal after it has been tanned, or softened; for use in making shoes and other items.

lopsided (lop′ sī′ dəd) *adj.* One side is bigger than the other; leaning to one side.

lurk (lûrk) *v.* To move slowly and quietly without being noticed.

M

mallard (ma′ lərd) *n.* A wild duck.

manner (ma′ nər) *n.* A way of acting or behaving.

mimicry (mim′ i krē) *n.* Camouflage that makes an animal look like another kind of animal.

missionary (mish′ ə ner′ ē) *n.* A person who teaches religion to people of different beliefs.

muffle (mu′ fəl) *v.* To cover or surround.

mulish (myōō′ ləsh) *adj.* Being stubborn.

multiply (mul′ tə plī′) *v.* To greatly increase in number.

> **Pronunciation Key:** at; lāte; câre; fäther; set; mē; it; kīte; ox; rōse; ô in bought; coin; bŏŏk; tōō; form; out; up; use; turn; ə sound in about, chicken, pencil, cannon, circus; chair; hw in which; ring; shop; thin; thère; zh in treasure.

N

nab (nab) *v.* To grab and hold; to catch.

natural (na´ chə rəl) *adj.* Acting on information one is born with.

nimble (nim´ bəl) *adj.* Able to move easily; light on one's feet.

nip (nip) *v.* To bite or sting with cold.

notion (nō´ shən) *n.* Idea.

O

ordeal (or dēl´) *v.* A stressful time or event.

overalls (ō´ vər ôlz´) *n.* Loose trousers with a bib front and straps at the shoulders.

P

pack-ice (pak´ īs´) *n.* Sea ice that forms when pieces of floating ice get crushed together.

page (pāj) *n.* A boy servant.

palace (pal´ is) *n.* A large, fancy house; the home of a king and queen.

particular (pər ti´ kyə lər) *adj.* Being one single thing.

patient (pā´ shənt) *adj.* Calm; willing to wait; able to put up with a bad situation without complaining.

patterns (pat´ ərnz) *n.* Repeated shapes or colors on an animal.

peculiar (pə kyōōl´ yər) *adj.* Strange or different.

peeper (pē´ pər) *n.* Eye.

perform (pər form´) *v.* To act, sing, or dance in front of others.

perspire (pər spīr´) *v.* To sweat.

persuade (pər swād´) *v.* To convince someone to do or believe something.

pier (pēr) *n.* Something built from the shore out into water to be used as a landing or walkway.

plaid (plad) *n.* A pattern of overlapping squares, rectangles, and lines.

plankton (plangkʹ tən) *n.* A kind of very small plant life in a body of water.

plight (plīt) *n.* A bad situation.

plunge (plunj) *v.* To dive down into the water.

polish (poʹ ləsh) *v.* To make smooth and shiny by rubbing.

polka dot (pōʹ kə dotʹ) *n.* A pattern of solid colored circles.

porcupine (porʹ kyə pīn) *n.* An animal with stiff pointy bristles.

porcupine

pound (pound) *v.* To beat very hard.

predator (preʹ də tər) *n.* One who hunts for food.

preserve (pri zûrvʹ) *v.* To keep or save for the future.

prey (prā) *n.* One who is hunted as food.

project (proʹ jekt) *n.* A task.

protective (prə tekʹ tiv) *adj.* Keeps out of danger or away from harm.

ptarmigan (tarʹ mi gən) *n.* A bird that changes feathers from dark in the summer to white in the winter.

pteranodon (tə raʹ nə don) *n.* A flying dinosaur.

Q

quill (kwil) *n.* A stiff pointy bristle on a porcupine.

quilt (kwilt) *v.* To sew layers of fabric together to make a cover for a bed.

Pronunciation Key: at; lāte; câre; fäther; set; mē; it; kīte; ox; rōse; ô in bought; coin; bŏŏk; tōō; form; out; up; use; turn; ə sound in about, chicken, pencil, cannon, circus; chair; hw in which; ring; shop; thin; *th*ere; zh in treasure.

R

reply (ri plī´) *v.* To answer.

rounds (roundz) *n.* The same trip taken over and over; a route taken that begins each time in the same place.

rustle (ru´ səl) *v.* To make a soft noise with little movement.

S

search (sûrch) *v.* To look for.

Sequoyah (si kwoi´ ə) *n.* The person who created a way to write the Cherokee language.

shoemaker (shōō´ mā´ kər) *n.* A person who makes or repairs shoes.

shopper (shop´ ər) *n.* A person who is looking for things to buy.

shrubby (shru´ bē) *adj.* Filled out with leaves and limbs; bushy.

sigh (sī) *v.* To let out a loud breath.

silversmith (sil´ vər smith´) *n.* Someone who makes objects from silver.

skedaddle (ski da´ dəl) *v.* To leave quickly; run away.

skim (skim) *v.* To pass over quickly, just barely touching the surface.

skitter (ski´ tər) *v.* To glide quickly.

sky-crane (skī´ krān) *n.* A machine that uses cables to lift and move heavy objects.

slink (slingk) *v.* To move quietly, slowly, and close to the ground; to creep.

slither (sli´ *th*ər) *v.* To slide like a reptile without arms or legs.

slop (slop) *v.* To feed.

sniff (snif) *v.* To smell; to draw a short breath up the nose.

sofa (sō´ fə) *n.* A couch with a back and two arms.

solitary (so´ lə târ ē) *adj.* Being alone.

spatter (spa´ tər) *v.* To splash with small drops.

splutter (splu´ tər) *v.* To say with a splashing sound.

squashed (skwôshd) *adj.* Looking flat.

squat (skwôt) *adj.* Short and thick.

squid (skwid) *n.* A sea animal with a tube-shaped body and ten arms.

squid

stalk (stôk) *n.* The main stem of a plant.

steady (ste´ dē) *v.* To make feel strong and sure.

steep (stēp) *adj.* Almost straight up-and-down.

stubborn (stu´ bərn) *adj.* Not willing to change one's mind.

stubby (stu´ bē) *adj.* Short and thick.

stumble (stum´ bəl) *v.* To make a mistake.

supermarket (soo´ pər mär´ kət) *n.* A store in which a person can choose food and household items to buy.

surface (sûr´ fəs) *n.* The top part of something.—*v.* To come up to the surface.

surroundings (sə roun´ dingz) *n.* The objects around an animal.

swoop (swoop) *v.* To fly down then back up quickly.

syllabary (si´ lə ber´ ē) *n.* A series of written characters, each of which stands for a syllable.

syllable (sil´ ə bəl) *n.* A letter or group of letters that make one sound when spoken.

T

tangle (tang´ gəl) *v.* To get twisted around.

tasseled (ta´ səld) *adj.* Looking like a tassel, which is a bunch of strings tied at one end.

Pronunciation Key: at; lāte; câre; fäther; set; mē; it; kīte; ox; rōse; ô in bought; coin; bŏŏk; tōō; form; out; up; use; turn; ə sound in about, chicken, pencil, cannon, circus; chair; hw in which; ring; shop; thin; thëre; zh in treasure.

temperature (tem´ pə chər´) *n.* A measure of how warm or cold something is.

tender (ten´ dər) *adj.* Soft and gentle.

thicket (thi´ kət) *n.* An area overgrown with small trees, bushes, and weeds.

top hat (top´ hat´) *n.* A man's hat that has a tall top shaped like a tube.

toppled (to´ pəld) *adj.* Overturned.

tote (tōt) *v.* To carry.

trader (trā´ dər) *n.* Someone who exchanges goods with others.

tradition (trə dish´ ən) *n.* A belief or custom that is passed on from old to young.

trout (trout) *n.* A long bony fish.

trudge (truj) *v.* To walk with great effort.

twitch (twich) *v.* To move with a jerk.

U

unaware (ən´ ə wâr´) *adv.* Not knowing what is happening.

uncertain (ən´ sûr´ tən) *adj.* Not sure.

V

view (vyōō) *n.* Objects within one's sight.

W

wand (wond) *n.* A magic rod; a stick that is used for magic.

wariest (wâr´ ē əst) *adj.* Superlative of **wary:** Having a feeling that danger may be near; watching for danger.

warrior (wôr´ ē ər) *n.* Someone who fights battles.

watchman (woch´ mən) *n.* A man whose job is to guard property.

waterspout (wô´ tər spout´) *n.* A stream of water that shoots from a whale's blowhole when it comes to the surface for air.

whir (hwûr) *v.* To fly quickly, making a noise with wings.

whirlwind (hwûrl´ wind´) *n.* Wind that moves in a circle with great force.

whoosh (hwo͞osh) *v.* To move quickly, stirring things up.

wondrous (wun´ drəs) *adj.* Wonderful; amazing.

Y

yip (yip) *v.* To make a short high-pitched sound.

Z

zodiac (zō´ dē ak´) *n.* Groups of stars.

Photo Credits

10, ©Tom & Pat Leeson/DRK Photo; **62(b),** © SYS, Japan; **86(t),** © Arte Publico Press; **86(b),** © Bernd Noble; **90,** © Philadelphia Museum of Art/Corbis; **92,** © Bill Terry/The Viesti Collection, Inc.; **99,** © Bill Terry/The Viesti Collection, Inc.; **101,** © Library of Congress/Corbis; **103,** © The National Archives/Corbis; **105,** © Rare Books Division/The New York Public Library/Astor, Lenox and Tilden Foundations; **107,** © SuperStock; **108,** © Joe Englander/The Viesti Collection, Inc.; **109,** © Lawrence Migdale; **112,** © Kotoh/ Zefa/H. Armstrong Roberts; **144,** © JP & Co.; **292,** © Darrell Gulin/DRK Photo; **293,** © Tom Till/DRK Photo; **294,** © Fred Bruemmer/DRK Photo; **295,** © M.C. Chamberlain/DRK Photo; **296,** © James P. Rowan/DRK Photo; **297,** © Tom & Pat Leeson/DRK Photo; **298,** © Andy Rouse/DRK Photo; **299,** © Tom & Pat Leeson/ Photo Researchers, Inc.; **300,** © C.C. Lockwood/Animals Animals; **301,** © Larry Mishkar/Dembinsky Photo Associates; **302,** © Rod Planck/Photo Researchers, Inc.; **303,** © Wayne Lankinen/DRK Photo; **304,** © Stan Wayman/Photo Researchers, Inc.; **305,** © Leonard Lee Rue III//DRK Photo; **306,** © Wayne Lankinen/DRK Photo; **307,** © Gary R. Zahm/DRK Photo; **308,** © Gilbert S. Grant/Photo Researchers, Inc.; **309,** © Joe McDonald/DRK Photo; **310,** © M.H. Sharp/Photo Researchers, Inc.; **311,** © Ray Coleman/Photo Researchers, Inc.; **312,** © Bruce Watkins/Animals Animals; **313,** © Tom McHugh/Photo Researchers, Inc.; **314,** © John Bova/Photo Researchers, Inc.; **315,** © David M. Schleser/Photo Researchers, Inc.

Art Acknowledgments

Unit 1 (Sharing Stories) Bill Ogden
Unit 2 (Kindness) Sucie Stevenson
Unit 3 (Look Again) Dara Goldman